"Building a great sales team starts with sales leaders who have self-awareness and effective sales management skills. Whether you're hiring young talent or experienced salespeople, this book provides exceptional tools and stories that prepare your company for greater sales growth and less stagnant sales cultures."
—Eric Taylor, Director, Global Talent Management, Gallagher

"As a previous sales leader and now CEO, I know how sales management has become one of the most challenging aspects of growing a business. Business has evolved with the application of new technologies, but sales management is still reliant on interpersonal, human connections. This book shows leaders how to teach and apply empathy, humility, and accountability. A must-read!"
—Karen Short, CEO, Universal Companies

"This is another great book by Colleen Stanley. The focus on improving emotional intelligence skills will help sales leaders take a different approach to traditional sales management practices. I'm recommending this book to my students, fellow sales educators, and sales leaders."
—Yashar Atefi, Director, Sales Leadership Center,
Daniels College of Business, University of Denver

"Colleen is masterful at guiding us through the application of emotional intelligence skills such as empathy, assertiveness, and emotion management needed in our role as sales managers. This book gives pragmatic tools for creating emotionally intelligent sales teams that will excel in sales beyond their wildest dreams!"
—Polly Lestikow, President, Closet Factory Colorado

"Reading this book was the next best thing to attending Colleen's sales management workshop. Clear and candid, she has you nodding all the way through the book, remembering your own experiences with instant-gratification sellers or trigger-response-regret moments. I'm excited to use the many insights and tools with my team!"
—Stephanie Medina, Regional Sales Manager, LinkedIn

EMOTIONAL INTELLIGENCE

INTELLIGENCE

FOR

SALES

LEADERSHIP

EMOTIONAL INTELLIGENCE

FOR

SALES LEADERSHIP

The Secret to Building
High-Performance Sales Teams

Colleen Stanley

HarperCollins
LEADERSHIP

AN IMPRINT OF HARPERCOLLINS

Published by HarperCollins Leadership, an imprint of HarperCollins Focus LLC.

Book design by Maria Fernandez for Neuwirth & Associates.

ISBN 978-1-4002-1773-1 (eBook)
ISBN 978-1-4002-1772-4 (TP)

Library of Congress Control Number: 2020931362

This book is dedicated to our great clients.
Every week at SalesLeadership, we comment on our good fortune
of working with such smart, humble, hardworking salespeople
and sales leaders. You are simply the best.

To sales leaders all over the world, hats off to you.
Your dedication to developing salespeople and helping clients inspires me
to continue on the journey of continuous improvement.

CONTENTS

Acknowledgments

I OFTEN SHARE THAT it takes a sales village to win and retain business. It also takes a sales village to write and publish a book. I've been very blessed to be surrounded by some great "villagers."

As you'll learn through the various stories shared in this book, Varsity Spirit was and is still a part of my village. They gave me my first opportunities in sales and sales leadership, which launched me into my current career of teaching and speaking about sales and sales leadership. Thank you.

An important person in the SalesLeadership village is Julie Points. She is my right arm, wing woman, and sales development manager. We call her the "super glue" of SalesLeadership because of her incredible organization and dedication to helping everyone succeed, from our consultants to our clients.

To my many colleagues at Women Sales Pros, thank you for being a part of my village. Jill Konrath started this group years ago, and many of us are graduates of Jill's "kick butt" program. My first book, *Emotional Intelligence For Sales Success*, would not have happened without her encouragement. (Okay . . . and hard push.) The success of that book led to the writing of this book.

This generous group of speakers, trainers, and consultants provided me with insight, support, and *many* moments of laughter. Nancy Bleeke and Lynn Hidy, thanks for reviewing book chapters and shining a light on gaps in content or thoughts.

Thanks to the HarperCollins team for believing in this topic. I recognize that publishers are approached by hundreds of authors each year and am grateful your team believed in this topic. I look forward to our continuing partnership and spreading the good word of emotional intelligence and sales leadership.

The earliest members of my village were the many great teachers that influenced me early in life. Sister Emma, Sister Nancy, Jan Gruber, and Martin Wedeking taught and modeled attributes of faith, honesty, perseverance, compassion, discipline, and generosity. Those teachings continue to guide me today.

My wonderful husband, Jim, is a key member of the village. He's my biggest cheerleader, never complains about a sometimes-crazy work or travel schedule. He is one of the good guys.

Why Emotional Intelligence Matters in Building High-Performance Sales Organizations

MUCH HAS BEEN WRITTEN on how competitive things have gotten in the world of sales. The bad news is that it's only going to get more competitive with the impact of technology, artificial intelligence, and a global economy. Successful companies always look for new and better ways to disrupt their market and serve their clients. They invest their money in improving technology platforms to ensure that products and services are delivered in the fastest, most convenient manner for clients. More dollars are spent on branding and marketing, trying to win the attention of prospects in a busy, distracted, 24/7 world.

These are all certainly a wise use of resources, but there is one more approach to winning business that is often overlooked by many sales organizations. That approach is to fully incorporate emotional intelligence into your hiring strategies, sales training methodologies, and sales leadership practices.

I am sure there are some sales leaders reading this and shaking their heads, wondering how soft skills, emotional intelligence skills, can produce hard sales results. Rather than pontificate on the benefits of emotional intelligence, let me ask if you've experienced any of the following challenges in your role as a sales leader.

- Your sales team is discounting, selling on price, even when your company offers a better value. And this is after you've enrolled your sales team in a negotiation skills workshop.
- Your title is vice president of sales or sales manager but some days you feel like your business card should read kindergarten teacher or psychotherapist. Daily sales drama eats up too much of your valuable time.
- Your sales team talks too much and listens too little, even though you've taught them a great questioning model.
- You've emphasized the importance of salespeople offering new insights and new ways of thinking to prospects. But your sales team can't share any insights because they aren't motivated to learn them.
- You were a top sales producer but your sales team isn't embracing what you teach and coach. You're wondering if it's you or them.
- The sales team is hiding behind email and text communication rather than talking to live, human beings.

Some of these challenges occur because of ineffective selling skills. And many, as you will learn in this book, are due to a lack of soft skills, emotional intelligence skills.

Learning and applying emotional intelligence skills in your day-to-day role as a sales manager will dramatically reduce or eliminate the sales management challenges mentioned above. It's time for a new perspective. It's time to incorporate emotional intelligence into your sales leadership processes.

The Sales Leadership Insanity Loop

We live in the information age. Salespeople and sales managers have access to more selling tools and knowledge than ever before to be successful. We can listen to sales podcasts, attend webinars or live sales training and management courses, and read informative blogs.

But according to CSO Insights, the research arm of Miller Heiman, achievement of quota for salespeople continues to hover around 53 percent. Why? There isn't one answer. However, in my work with hundreds of sales organizations, I find the biggest reason is that sales organizations work on the wrong end of the problem when faced with sales performance issues. They are stuck in the insanity loop of sales management, one where they keep repeating the same mistakes over and over.

- **Sales managers only vet new candidates for their industry experience and selling skills**—what I refer to as the hard skills, Sales IQ. But they don't interview for soft skills, emotional intelligence skills, Sales EQ. As a result, sales managers hire culture misfits that wreak havoc on the company culture and core values. Your new hire is great at selling but not great at playing well in the sandbox with others.

- **When a salesperson misses sales quota, a sales manager's first response is to teach more hard-selling skills, consultative selling skills.** These skills are important, and we teach a lot of them. But is the salesperson not asking enough questions during a sales call because he doesn't know the questions to ask? Or, is it because he needs to learn better impulse control and self-awareness to understand when and how he gets triggered during a meeting resulting in a product dump?

The best sales teams are led by sales leaders who teach, coach, and master both the consultative selling skills (Sales IQ) and soft skills (Sales EQ) to accelerate sales results.

Where's the Proof?

Research conducted by the Corporate Executive Board uncovered key traits found in the most successful salespeople. One of the traits found in the most successful salespeople is the skill of assertiveness. But assertiveness is not a hard-selling skill, a consultative selling skill. It's an emotional intelligence skill, one that helps a salesperson state what she needs nicely in sales conversations to create partnerships, not "vendor-ship" relationships. Assertiveness is the soft skill that supports the consistent execution of hard-selling skills, helping a salesperson say and do the right things during a sales call.

Steven Stein and Howard Book, authors of *The EQ Edge*, have collected extensive research from their work with successful CEOs and leaders. Not surprising, their data shows that the most profitable leaders consistently score high in two emotional intelligence skills: empathy and self-regard. Empathetic leaders are good listeners. They have the ability to read the emotional temperature of their employees. Their ability to connect and relate to their teams helps them retain top talent, avoiding the high cost of turnover.

Leaders possessing high self-regard are aware of their strengths and weaknesses. This awareness and confidence helps them avoid blind spots that derail good decision-making and careers. Sales teams like and trust these leaders because they have no problem quickly admitting when they make a mistake. Vulnerability and honesty build trust, great teams, and profitability. But how many sales leaders have engaged in training or coaching to develop their emotional intelligence skills? The answer is not enough.

Why Read This Book?

For too long, hardworking salespeople and sales managers have not earned what they are worth. Salespeople get flustered on sales calls because emotions, rather than effective sales and influence skills, start running the meeting. Many forget to bring important soft skills to a sales conversation, blowing the sales meeting in the first five minutes because they aren't reading the emotional temperature of their prospect or customer.

> **Low self-awareness = low other awareness =
> no connection = no sale**

On the other side of the sales equation, I've encountered sales-people earning big money—accompanied by great stress. They don't enjoy the sales profession as much as they could due to their lack of emotional intelligence skills. They fall into the trap of working harder-not-smarter, which leads to fatigue, burnout, and dropout. Both scenarios create unnecessary turnover, forcing sales managers to spend more time interviewing new salespeople than time developing their current sales team.

It's the insanity loop!

Sales managers get derailed coaching salespeople because emotions, not effective training and coaching skills, start running the coaching conversation. They aren't aware of how they show up to coaching conversations, often creating the defensive behaviors they dread when delivering well-intended feedback. Sales managers forget to bring empathy to a coaching conversation. They immediately dispense advice without thinking about the salesperson's emotional state around this particular sales performance challenge.

Sales and Sales Management Should Be Fun

We often spend more time at work than we do with our families. Developing your sales team's emotional intelligence skills makes your life as a sales leader easier and more enjoyable. Emotionally intelligent sales teams achieve the fun quota *and* the sales quota. These sales teams learn and master the soft skills, ones that often aren't taught in grade school, high school—and certainly not in traditional sales training or sales management training. Skills such as:

- Empathy and how to make emotional connections that accelerate trust, improve relationships, and increase closed business.
- Emotion management, which limits nonproductive fight-or-flight conversations with prospects, customers, and members of their own team.
- Stress management skills, which decrease frustration and increase productivity.
- Self-limiting belief systems that often rob salespeople of achieving their best in life.
- Self-awareness and other awareness, which eliminates repeated mistakes in building relationships and achieving sales goals.
- Embracing failure and feedback. Mastery is not achieved without feedback or failure, and improved self-regard skills improves the ability to accept both.

Emotionally intelligent people are refreshing people to work with because they don't get caught up in the game of blame and excuses. High EQ salespeople don't blame outside circumstances for their failures. They are competitive, confident, and humble salespeople who own their successes and their failures. These individuals are introspective, always asking the question, "What do I need to do to change, grow, and improve? How am I showing up in my relationships and conversations?"

It's time for a new perspective in sales and sales leadership. It's time to incorporate emotional intelligence skills into your sales hiring, training, and leadership processes.

Let's get started.

PART I

IT'S TIME FOR A NEW SALES LEADERSHIP PERSPECTIVE

I learned to always take on things I'd never done before.
Growth and comfort do not coexist.

—Ginni Rometty

It takes something more than intelligence to act intelligently.

—Fyodor Dostoyevsky

Welcome to an Emotionally Intelligent Sales Team and Meeting

PETE IS A NEW sales manager and excited about leading and developing his sales team. At the same time, he is a little nervous because he is new and has enough self-awareness to recognize that he doesn't know what he doesn't know.

He reaches out to Victoria, a longtime colleague and informal mentor. She has been a successful sales manager for over ten years and still loves her role as a sales leader.

Victoria invites Pete to her biweekly group sales meeting to observe. Upon entering the room. Pete immediately notices that something is different, but he can't quite put his finger on it. Then he gets it: the salespeople are talking to one another. They aren't checking their smartphones or tablets for emails. Instead, they are fully present with their peers, engaging in relationship-building. Salespeople located outside of the corporate office are doing the same thing via videoconferencing, talking and joking with peers. This is weird . . . don't these salespeople have prospects and clients pinging them? Shouldn't they be multitasking? Isn't there something that needs their immediate attention?

The meeting starts and Pete notices that the team is following a preset agenda. He makes a note that having an agenda is probably a good idea. It's similar to running a productive sales call where you and the prospect know the defined purpose and objective of the call.

Victoria starts the meeting with the same question she asks at the beginning of each sales meeting: "What are we doing right?" Pete looks around the room and now he's really confused. "Aren't these sales meetings for problem solving? Why is Victoria wasting time on this feel-good question? Shouldn't she get the team focused on addressing operational issues or client concerns?"

The sales team responds enthusiastically, reporting personal and company success stories. Pete feels the optimism and enthusiasm rising in the room. He sees the pride on their faces, because the sales team recognizes they are on a winning team, a great team.

Victoria moves to the next point on the agenda and teaches the sales team a new concept for conducting more thoughtful sales conversations. Only one concept is presented, and the sales team organizes into practice pods. Pete listens closely to the role-plays. To his surprise, he doesn't hear the usual, "I don't want to role-play . . . this isn't real . . . I'm uncomfortable." Pete wonders where Victoria found these salespeople.

After several practice sets and debriefs, Victoria moves to the next agenda item. She asks the sales team, "With what part of the sales process are you having difficulty? Where are your deals getting stuck?" Pete waits for the silence. I mean, really, who wants to admit they aren't a sales rock star? To his amazement, several hands shoot up. But what's even more amazing is what he is hearing. The salespeople are admitting where and how they screwed up!

- "I really got outsold on my last deal . . . and the worst part is, I am not even sure how I got outsold! I need some help on this one."

- "I didn't get a piece of business that I really should have won. And the reason is, I failed to prepare. I need to own this loss. Let me tell you what I am going to do differently the next time in order to win."
- "I'm a little embarrassed to admit this but I'm feeling really intimidated by the size of this opportunity. I could use some help here to wrap my head around how to navigate through this selling scenario."

Pete's mind is racing. His experience in previous sales meetings has been a demonstration of the total opposite behaviors. Salespeople blame the company for their losses: not enough leads, need better marketing support, or the good old standby, our prices are too high. What is going on here? How did Victoria create this?

The final part of the meeting is a quick lap around the room and check-in with videoconference attendees. Each salesperson makes a commitment to one improvement in their sales process before the next meeting. Each salesperson finds an accountability partner on the team to conduct a daily check-in on progress toward their goals.

The meeting ends with everyone high-fiving each other and wishing each other good luck on their specific sales opportunities.

Pete thanks Victoria for the opportunity to observe the meeting. Driving back to his office, he wonders if actors were hired and the entire sales meeting was staged for his benefit.

At this point, Mr. or Ms. Reader, you might be thinking the same thing. No, the sales meeting wasn't staged. What Pete observed is an emotionally intelligent sales team. These teams are comprised of sales leaders and salespeople with high self-awareness and personal accountability. No finger-pointing or blame because they live by the old, kind of corny mantra, "If it is to be, it's up to me."

Emotionally intelligent sales teams understand the power of delayed gratification, putting in the work, the practice, to get better at their craft. They don't talk teamwork, they *do* teamwork, which starts with talking and building relationships with your teammates and helping them be successful.

This culture starts at the top. Emotionally intelligent sales teams are led by emotionally intelligent sales leaders. You don't have to be perfect to get started. I should know, as I am a work in progress, still trying to master the many aspects of emotional intelligence. The good news is that emotional intelligence can be improved with desire, commitment, and focus.

As the late author Maya Angelou said, "When you know better, you do better." If you're ready to do better in your sales leadership role, this book will help you on your journey.

To evaluate the emotional intelligence of your sales organization, go to www.EmotionalIntelligenceForSalesLeadership.com and take our Emotional Intelligence Sales Team assessment.

2

It All Starts with You

CONGRATULATIONS IF YOU'VE PICKED up this book because you've received a promotion to sales management. I am sure that promotion is well deserved because you have been a top salesperson for years, producing consistent and profitable sales results.

It could also be that you are a sales leader who's been leading sales teams for years and want to learn new ideas to motivate your team.

In either case, before you read any more pages, I'd like you to slow down and ask yourself if you really want to be a sales manager. Do you like sales management? I know this might sound like a crazy question but I've seen more than one salesperson accept a promotion to sales management that turned out to be a promotion to misery.

Years ago, I was hired by a company for a large engagement to provide our Ei Selling® program. After the training, this company opted for the sales managers to teach and reinforce all of the key learnings. Unfortunately, most of the sales managers failed miserably.

The biggest reason for failing was that many of the sales managers didn't like conducting consistent one-on-one coaching sessions with their teams. They were fully equipped with training tools to debrief sales calls, pre-brief sales calls, set up role-plays, and drill skills with their teams. But reinforcement takes time and these sales managers always gave in to the pull of instant gratification and kept prioritizing other things over coaching.

These sales managers weren't bad people. Like many successful salespeople, they'd accepted the role of sales management when they really preferred the role of a seller. These sales managers simply liked selling and closing deals better than they liked developing salespeople.

Know Thyself

Apply the emotional intelligence skill of self-awareness. Self-awareness is knowing and understanding yourself. It's the conscious knowledge of one's own feelings, motives, and desires. It's the mega soft skill, because that which you are not aware of you cannot change.

Carve out quiet time, ask and answer the following questions to make sure you want to take on—or continue—the role of sales leadership:

- Will/do you enjoy your new role as a sales leader as much as your role of an individual seller?
- Will/do you enjoy your current role as sales manager? What are possible blind spots that could be or are affecting your success as a sales leader?
- Are you willing to go through the steep learning curve required to learn the new set of skills (such as hiring,

training, coaching, and holding salespeople accountable) to lead a team?

If the answer is no, that's okay. I admire CFOs but I certainly don't want to be one. Know thyself.

Hiring and Selection Skills

Sales managers are promoted because of their business development skills. Many love the thrill of finding new opportunities, holding provocative sales conversations, and closing business deals. You are still prospecting in your role as a sales manager, but the target changes. You are now focused on prospecting for the best sales talent. Instead of qualifying prospects, you now have to fine-tune your interviewing skills to qualify potential sales candidates. Should this prospective candidate even be in your people pipeline? As a sales manager, the most important deals you'll close are the ones around hiring great salespeople.

Self-awareness questions: How energized are you about filling a salespeople pipeline? Are you as motivated by "hunting" for potential sales candidates as you are about identifying new prospects? What's your level of commitment toward learning new skills such as recruiting, running behavior-based interviews, reference checks, and vetting resumes? Are you as excited about closing a new sales hire as a new prospect?

Training and Coaching Skills

Jack Welch, former CEO of GE, says it best: "When you take on a leadership role, it's no longer about you, it's about them." You may have been a great seller but, unfortunately, your great selling skills are of no use or value if you can't transfer these skills, habits, and attitude to your sales team.

If I didn't enjoy teaching and coaching, I wouldn't have signed up for sales management or entered the field of speaking, training, and coaching. Teaching looks like a lot of fun—and it is. It also can be tedious, as mastery requires a lot of repetition and practice to elevate a salesperson's selling skills. The coaching sessions require a lot of patience.

Self-awareness questions: How jazzed are you about pre-briefing sales calls, debriefing sales calls, conducting role-plays, and more role-plays? Do you have the delayed gratification skills, the patience, to put in the work to develop salespeople? Would you rather be closing the deal yourself or teaching others how to do it? How motivated are you to put in the work to learn how to be a great teacher and coach?

Accountability

Great sales managers are comfortable setting high standards for the sales team and holding them accountable to metrics and outcomes. Sales leaders are always raising the bar of excellence because they know their best competitors are constantly raising the bar. But raising the bar can raise objections from the sales team. This pushback happens even when new goals, systems, or standards will help your sales team be more effective. Anyone reading this chapter still fighting the "I don't want to put it in my CRM" excuse? Salespeople are humans first—and as you will learn, human beings don't like change.

Accountability often requires having the tough-love, truth-telling conversations with salespeople and pointing out blind spots or not-so-blind spots. When you accept the role of sales management, you accept the role of growing people and profits. It's similar to being a good parent. The best parents understand that raising kids isn't a popularity contest and refuse to cave when their child says, "None of the other kids' moms expect them to . . . everyone else gets to . . ."

Self-awareness and reality testing questions: How comfortable are you holding salespeople accountable to metrics and outcomes? Do you have the self-confidence to stay the course when your sales team wants to take an easier, less productive course of action? How committed are you to learning the new feedback skills required to hold truth-telling coaching conversations?

Balancing People and Profits

My experience in working with hundreds of sales organizations has exposed me to different types of sales managers. Typically sales managers fall into one of three buckets: the field sales manager, the corporate sales manager, and the all-around sales manager.

Field sales managers are those sales leaders who stand by their sales team no matter what. They defend any and all actions of their sales team, refusing to understand or endorse corporate initiatives. They don't really understand or care how the company makes money. Field managers enjoy a lot of love from their sales team but also limit their company's growth and profits.

The corporate sales manager is . . . corporate. These sales managers never leave the comfort of their offices. They spend their time buried in reports, analyzing data, and attending internal meetings. Little or no time is invested in talking to their sales team. They are kind of like an athletic coach trying to coach a team from an air-conditioned suite, rather than on the field or on the court. Because they never leave the office, they are clueless about the real demands and needs of their prospects and customers.

The all-around sales manager "gets it." This sales leader achieves that hard balance of presenting the sales team's issues to fellow executives while communicating and enforcing corporate objectives to the sales team. They are good at managing up and down, earning trust and respect from all parties. The all-around sales manager is good at achieving the balance of managing people and profits.

Self-awareness questions: What type of sales manager are you? Do you enjoy achieving that fine balance of meeting company strategic initiatives and the real-world needs of your sales team? Are you committed to learning the new skills required for managing up and down?

Get Out of the Office

Many years ago, when I was vice president of sales, I was traveling with one of my top salespeople to meet an important customer in Florida. She was a terrific salesperson and on more than one occasion had asked if our company could offer a bundling option for our customers around a particular line of business. I was buried in other work and had given her the same answer without any action. "Yeah, that's a great idea."

Upon meeting with this customer, I asked why she wasn't purchasing a specific line of business from us and the customer responded that it was because one of our competitors offered a bundling option. I'll never forget the shocked look on my salesperson's face when I replied, "Oh, we have a bundling option as well." When I returned to the corporate office, I immediately put together a bundling option! That conversation was a great lesson for me. When I saw and heard firsthand that our client was taking her business elsewhere, it got my full attention. It made me realize that I was spending a little too much time in the "white house," the corporate office, and not enough time in front of clients.

I was humbled and reminded of the power of accompanying salespeople on calls. It's easy to get sucked into other demands but nothing is more important than meeting the people who write our paychecks—our customers.

Sales Process and Playbooks

A sales leader cannot scale revenues quickly without a duplicable sales process. Try constructing a building without blueprints. How many of you would feel confident purchasing a car where the manufacturer encouraged their staff to "do their own thing?" Unfortunately, it happens in sales organizations every day.

Study high-performance teams such as professional athletic teams and while you will have top athletes that have been playing the sport for years, every great sports team has a playbook, one that the players are expected to study and flawlessly execute. Can you imagine the response a rookie player would receive if he went up to the coach and said, "Hey, I'm more comfortable using the playbook that I was taught in college. Are you good with that, Coach?" That would be a very short conversation because professional coaches know you can't coach twenty different playbooks. And neither can sales managers.

I've seen more than one company hire a process-averse sales manager, one who doesn't believe in the power of a sales playbook. Their sales departments look like the Wild West because there are no defined metrics or approaches to winning the right business. Each salesperson is running his or her own playbook with varying results.

No defined playbook forces the sales team to enroll in the University of Hard Knocks. Most salespeople flunk out of this university, creating stagnant growth or excessive turnover.

I've also worked with sales managers who embrace process—they just didn't want to be the ones to document their company's sales process. I don't blame them. It's hard work; it's detailed work. Coaching and training are fun, but the reality is you can't coach and train unless you have a defined process from which to do so.

Sticking with the Script

Dan Flanagan is the chief sales officer for BluSky. They are a great success story as they have grown revenues from $20 million to $225 million in eight years and they are well on their way to $500 million.

This company does a lot of things right. They have a great sales culture—one they fiercely protect by hiring salespeople who play well with others and enjoy learning. They understand the power of team and they continue to invest big dollars in retreats and sales meetings to ensure their sales team is on the right page of their comprehensive sales playbook.

Dan learned the power of a sales playbook during his college years when he went door-to-door selling educational books for the Southwestern Company. Southwestern requires their young recruits to learn a script, and as Dan quickly learned, the successful sellers didn't deviate from it. The "dropouts" from the program usually wanted to execute their own scripts, which didn't achieve sales results. Dan took those early lessons into his role as chief sales officer, documenting his organization's best sales practices.

Augment your efforts by tapping into sales management resources. Suzanne Paling, author of *The Accidental Sales Manager*, shares a lot of great tools and templates in her book that will help get you started. You don't have to go it alone.

Self-awareness and reality testing questions: What is your attitude toward installing sales processes and systems? Have you invested the time to document scripts, questions, selling stages, and approaches? Do you rebel against process or embrace processes that can be measured, adapted, and changed? (If you don't want to be in charge of installing and documenting sales processes, that's okay. But do yourself a favor and stay or return to your role as a seller.)

Sales managers, it all starts with you. Sales leadership is rewarding, but only if the responsibilities of the job align with your strengths and motivators. Apply the emotional intelligence skill of self-awareness and make sure that you want to be a sales leader.

If your answer is still *yes* after reading this chapter, great! Let's dive into building a high-performance and emotionally intelligent sales team. There are three areas I will cover in this book:

1. Hiring and selecting emotionally intelligent salespeople.
2. Tools and tips for teaching your sales team the soft skills needed to win business and retain business.
3. Developing key emotional intelligence skills that will help you be a more effective sales coach and leader.

PART II

GET THIS RIGHT OR NOTHING ELSE MATTERS—HIRE FOR SALES EQ

I am convinced that nothing we do is more important than hiring and developing people. At the end of the day, you bet on people, not on strategies.

—Lawrence Bossidy

In a high-IQ job pool, soft skills like discipline, drive, and empathy mark those who emerge as outstanding.

—Daniel Goleman

3

Sales
Draft
Day

OKAY, YOU'VE MADE THE decision that you are up for the challenge and reward of sales leadership. You recognize the skills needed to lead and direct a sales team are very different than those needed to be a great salesperson. Sales leadership requires skills such as training and coaching, giving feedback, accountability, and running effective sales meetings. We'll get more into these skills in future chapters, but first let's talk about one more sales management skill you will need to master. Without this skill, *the rest doesn't matter.*

Learn how to hire great salespeople. It's the difference between hell and happiness in sales leadership. The golden rule in hiring is, "Past behavior is the best predictor of future sales results." It's a great rule to live by. Another rule: interview and hire for emotional intelligence.

When conducting our sales management hiring workshops, I open up with a fun exercise called, "Your worst sales hire." See Figure 3.1 for what bad hire stories usually include.

Negative attitude
Arrogant
Not coachable
Poor work ethic
No desire to learn
Not ethical
Bull in a china shop

FIGURE 3.1

This exercise creates an "ah-hah" moment because 90 percent of what participants share has nothing to do with selling skills. Failure to launch and culture misfits stem from lack of soft skills, emotional intelligence skills.

Sales EQ and Sales IQ

When we help sales organizations improve their hiring processes, we find that many are focused only on qualifying candidates for the hard skills, the Sales IQ competencies. These competencies range from number of years in sales to specific industry experience to size of deals that the salesperson closed. These criteria are very important—so don't eliminate these competencies in your selection process.

Equally important is interviewing and testing for emotional intelligence skills, *Sales EQ*. If you're serious about creating

great sales teams, great sales cultures, get serious about interviewing and eliminating candidates who are *not* a good culture fit. Get serious about hiring salespeople with emotional
intelligence.

You've all heard the phrase "One bad apple spoils the bunch."
This isn't just a cute phrase. Research shows that people will catch
and carry the mood of other human beings. It's called emotional
contagion. If you hire a whiner, excuse-maker, a poor team player,
you've just infused a negative virus into your sales culture, one that
spreads rapidly.

The Bad Apple

When I was in my twenties, I was a buyer for a chain of stores
located in Nebraska. We had a good team environment until
a woman I will call Beth joined the company. In the beginning, she seemed like a lot of fun. But slowly, she started
complaining about everything. She complained about our
boss, company policies, travel requirements. And pretty
soon, I am sorry to say, the rest of us joined in her sad
chorus. Workdays were filled with complaints rather than
our former good energy and humor. The focus slowly turned
to everything we lacked rather than all the good things the
company had in place. Internal bickering started because
negativity breeds negativity. Looking back, I wish I had the
emotional intelligence skills to recognize that I was catching
a virus, one of complaining and whining. One bad sales apple
can indeed spoil a good culture.

It's Draft Day

My husband and I love watching movies. We get absorbed in great movie plots that provide escape and entertainment. Often, when watching movies, I see overarching themes that can be applied to sales and sales management success. I know . . . not proud of this behavior but it's kind of the way my brain is wired.

Draft Day is a movie that I recommend to all my sales managers who want to improve their hiring practices. Kevin Costner plays the character of Sonny Weaver, who is the fictional general manager of the Cleveland Browns. The plot revolves around what to do after his team acquires the number one draft pick in the upcoming National Football League draft. Everyone should be happy, right? Instead, the plot takes a turn when Weaver assigns his coaching team to find the "something" this talented quarterback *doesn't* possess. Sonny shares his recruiting philosophy with his coaching staff. "Everyone has 'something' missing, 'something' to work on. I need you to find this recruit's 'something' because I need to figure out if I can live with it or not."

Sonny Weaver was applying the EQ skill of reality testing, which is the ability to see things for what they are rather than what you'd like them to be. How many of you have made the mistake of falling in love with your candidate so you stopped searching for that "something?" Your love affair with a candidate causes you to shortcut the hiring process.

Sonny's mindset, searching for "something," is a best practice that all sales managers should adopt in their hiring practices. Sales leaders hire and work with human beings. The last time I checked, human beings are not perfect. They show up with flaws and blind spots. When interviewing candidates, continue to ask yourself the three questions in Figure 3.2.

- **What is this candidate's something?**

- **Can I live with this something?**

- **Do I have time, patience, and resources to help the salesperson improve on the something?**

FIGURE 3.2

Get Clear on Your Nonnegotiables

Dave Ramsey is the CEO of a multimillion-dollar company, radio show host, and author of *EntreLeadership*. In his book, he shares his twelve steps to making a good hire. He encourages readers to get very clear on their core values, their nonnegotiables. One of his company's nonnegotiables is a huge work ethic. To paraphrase Dave, "Lazy is not a personality style. It's a character flaw."

Think about how hiring people with a huge work ethic might be challenged in today's business environment. Most companies seem to hide the desire for a strong work ethic. Their recruiting ads are full of promises of beer Friday and ping-pong tables. No wonder they attract salespeople who come in late and leave early. The salesperson thought she was interviewing for a position at a laid-back spa, not at a company where big work ethic is expected and rewarded.

Tony Dungy, former NFL Super Bowl coach, was very clear on his nonnegotiables. In his book *The One Year Uncommon Life Daily Challenge*, he talks about the evaluation process of new prospects while he was the coach of the Indianapolis Colts. They might have a player with plenty of experience, talent, and skills—all the hard athletic skills that looked like they were a perfect fit for the team. Even with all these marvelous qualifications, a candidate might be dismissed if he had DNDC written next to his name on the evaluation form. Do Not Draft (because of) Character. Tony and his staff were clear on their nonnegotiables. The soft skills of character were just as important to Coach Dungy as the hard skills of playing great football. He and his staff were clear on their one thing and would not recruit a player who demonstrated lack of integrity.

When we create hiring playbooks, we press clients to identify their nonnegotiables. Getting clear on your nonnegotiables requires self-awareness and introspection. We've all been raised to be nice people. And nice people are taught to give other people the benefit of the doubt. This type of thinking often leads to sales managers making poor decisions and not standing firm on disqualifying candidates who don't pass their nonnegotiables test.

Sales leaders, this is your sales organization. Get clear about what's important to you. You may think you're being nice. But if you are like me, my nice side quickly disappears when a salesperson breaches a nonnegotiable. It's not the salesperson's fault. It's mine because I didn't honor what's important to me in the hiring process.

Each sales organization's nonnegotiables vary because every sales organization has a different set of driving values, a different set of competencies needed to drive success at the life cycle of their company. Sales managers have different leadership styles, which create different "somethings" that are important to them.

Apply self-awareness and reality testing. Get clear on your nonnegotiables. Get clear on what you will or will not accept in a sales candidate.

Red Flags, Fires, and Self-Awareness

Sales managers miss "something" because they ignore "something." Anyone besides me been guilty of ignoring a red flag? After you hire the salesperson, the red flag turns into a big fire!

Time to apply the EQ skill of self-awareness. *That which you are not aware of you cannot change.* In reflecting on some of my hiring mistakes, I've recognized red flags that were ignored for a variety of reasons:

- *Exhaustion.* I was overwhelmed and needed help. I'd already invested my limited time identifying, interviewing, and calling references. When a red flag appeared, I didn't want to start over.
- *I didn't follow my own advice.* My salespeople pipeline was empty so I settled for a warm body, anybody!
- *Love.* It's easy to fall in love with a charming candidate's personality. This love affair leads to rationalizing or glossing over nonnegotiables. One of my nonnegotiables is learning and hiring learners. I remember hiring a very charming salesperson. During the interview, I asked him a question about the last business book he'd read. He smiled and said, "Well, I'm going to get an F on that answer. I've been so busy selling, I haven't had time to read." I accepted and rationalized his answer. Of course, he's selling and closing business! Now that he's working for a sales education firm, he will change his ways! He didn't. If you tend to fall in love easily, include someone in your hiring process who doesn't! An analytical person can be a great asset in hiring because of their ability to look for data in the answers exchanged in a live interview.
- *Logic over intuition.* You've got a nagging feeling about a candidate; however, you can't really put a finger on what's

making you uncomfortable. Since there is no evidence, some sales managers feel uncomfortable disqualifying a candidate. They want to be fair in the selection process. Take some advice from a colleague of mine who is a psychologist: "Don't wait for evidence to honor your intuition."

My colleague Beth Smith, author of *Why Can't I Hire Good People*, shares a great analogy that illustrates the problem of ignoring "something":

> It's similar to getting a small pebble in your shoe. Initially, it's not too bad, however, after a few hours of walking with that pebble in your shoe, it becomes irritating. After a few days, it feels like a rock and really hurts. The same happens when you hire the wrong person. What starts out as a small irritation ends up being a big rock in your shoe.

What pebbles and red flags have you ignored?

Remember, the difference between hell and happiness in sales management is getting the right people on your sales bus. Get clear on your "something." Don't ignore the red flags that turn into fires. Apply self-awareness and look at your blind spots when hiring.

EQ Action Steps for Sales Leaders

1. Review your current hiring processes and examine your interview questions. Are you vetting potential candidates for emotional intelligence skills (Sales EQ) and consultative selling skills (Sales IQ)?

2. Identify your nonnegotiables. Design interview questions to specifically uncover whether or not your candidates possess these traits.

3. Analyze previous poor hires to determine what red flags you ignored during the hiring process. Ask yourself the tough questions on why you ignored these red flags. That which you are not aware of you are bound to repeat.

4

Marshmallow Grabbers
and
Cookie Monsters

IN 1960, DR. WALTER Mischel, author of *The Marshmallow Test, Why Self-Control Is the Engine of Success*, became famous for what is now known as the "Marshmallow Study." He and his Stanford University research team wanted to understand willpower, specifically delayed gratification and how this skill could impact a person's future success. The participants in this research project were four-year-olds. The Cliff Notes version of this research is that he and his team would test a child's self-control by placing a treat, often a marshmallow, in front of a child with the promise that if they didn't eat the treat, the child would earn another treat. They found that the children who were able to demonstrate self-control and avoid gobbling down the treat immediately enjoyed more success in both their business and personal lives.

Many years later, Dr. Mischel was asked to consult with the Education and Research Group at Sesame Workshop. He worked with the *Sesame Street* team to create shows focused on teaching the importance of self-control. Their goal was to teach young viewers how to control themselves, especially in difficult situations.

The subject matter expert chosen to deliver this message was the Cookie Monster, a blue character best known for his frequent "Me want a cookie" requests. When cookies are not available, the Cookie Monster's appetite allows him to eat virtually anything else, including normally inedible objects. This character is a clear demonstration of the implications of low self-control and instant gratification.

I laughed out loud when I read about this character because there is a little bit of the Cookie Monster in all of us in the sales profession. "Me wants a full sales pipeline now. Me wants a sale now. Me wants to be masterful at sales now."

So, what does the Cookie Monster and instant gratification have to do with hiring good salespeople? A lot.

Delayed Gratification and Sales Results

When interviewing sales candidates, probe salespeople for their self-control and delayed gratification skills. These salespeople have the ability to put in the work to create successful sales outcomes. Instant gratification salespeople, "Me want it now" salespeople, have a hard time staying the course toward achieving goals. They gravitate toward the paths in life that promise a magic shortcut to success.

There are several areas of the sales process that are negatively impacted if you hire a cookie monster or a marshmallow grabber. Here are four I've consistently seen in working with sales teams.

Prospecting. Your company's sales cycle ranges from six to nine months from first contact to close. You're onboarding your new hire and establish the sales activity plan required to build a robust sales pipeline.

Your new salesperson is motivated to succeed. She consistently hits all sales activity metrics for the first three months. Deals are moving forward in the sales process but no business has closed. Frustration and the desire for instant gratification kick in, even though the salesperson knows that the sales cycle is six to nine months. "Me wants a sale now" thinking and selling behaviors set in.

She checks out and checks into instant gratification, non-revenue sales activity. She checks her social media sites, looking for likes and comments from strangers who can't or won't do business with her. She schedules coffees with other instant gratification salespeople where they commiserate on the difficulties of the sales profession. They validate each other's excuses for not doing the hard work of prospecting. "I've just got a bad territory."

Instant gratification salespeople settle for an instant gratification prospecting approach. Crafting compelling and customized prospecting messages takes time and effort. But instant gratification salespeople cave into "Me wants results now." They take the easy path, using generic, one-size-fits-all value propositions and approaches in their outbound prospecting efforts. They don't invest time designing messages specific to the buyer persona. Generic efforts equal dismal sales results because busy and educated prospects expect a salesperson to quickly demonstrate she knows and understands their business challenges and goals.

I asked one of my clients, Jimmy Malloy, a very successful financial planner, the keys to his success. He smiled his big Irish smile. "That's easy. You've got to do your first year sometime. And most salespeople never put in the work to do their first year."

Sales Skill Development. Delayed gratification is essential in mastering new selling skills and habits. Great salespeople practice a lot. As a result, they show up to sales meetings confident, relaxed, and prepared. They are fully present because they aren't wondering about their next sales ninja move or question. They *know* their next question because they've put in the time to practice and role-play. Mastery of selling skills is what allows a salesperson to truly listen instead of forming the next question without hearing the prospect's answer.

The Diamond in the Rough

I remember a client from my early years in this business. Ralph was what you'd call a little rough around the edges, not the most polished individual. But what Ralph lacked in polish, he made up for in delayed gratification skills. He always put in the work to be successful. When attending our workshops, he showed up prepared with questions, asking for advice on upcoming sales meetings or past sales conversations. Most important, he applied the coaching.

He would practice, practice, and practice some more. It was quite rewarding to see this rough-around-the-edges salesperson become a diamond and one of the top salespeople at his company.

Instant gratification salespeople excel at being average because they don't put in the work to achieve sales mastery. You can't afford to hire average because today's customers have too many choices and options. They simply don't write checks to average salespeople.

Major account selling. I've observed more than one sales manager waste precious time trying to train and coach a cookie monster salesperson on the mechanics of selling to major accounts.

Great sales training is imparted around identifying buying influences and how to conduct thoughtful sales conversations. Discussions are held around the best tactics and strategies to unseat the incumbent. Brainstorming sessions are conducted on how to get a foot in the door.

Here's the reality. Elephant hunting takes time and delayed gratification skills. Big accounts require more pre-call planning to figure out the buying landscape. Big accounts require more meetings with multiple decision makers. Big accounts often take longer to close because of the size or complexity of the deal.

The instant gratification salesperson knows what to do from the good training she received from her sales manager. But the salesperson continues to pursue smaller deals because they are easier to close. She gives into the pull of instant gratification and "Me wants a deal now" thinking. Sales leaders, if you need your team landing bigger accounts, interview potential candidates for delayed gratification skills.

Job-hopping. Shirley is a sales manager and is reviewing a stack of resumes. She notices that a lot of the potential sales candidates have changed jobs every two years. But she's also heard that salespeople aren't staying with one company anymore. Many will have as many as thirteen jobs in their lifetime. Shirley, like many sales managers, wonders if it's okay to settle for a job-hopper.

Don't do it.

Forget about what you've read on the internet, heard from thought leaders, or read in the paper. They've probably never hired a salesperson in their life! Or, they've given into the pull of instant gratification, settling for below-average salespeople.

Job-hopping salespeople tend to be instant gratification salespeople. When the going gets tough, they get going! These folks live in the world of "the grass is always greener on the other side of the fence." They don't put in the work making the grass greener at their current company.

I'm not going to share any research on this topic. Instead, I'll ask you to apply common sense and your own life experience. Look at successful colleagues and peers. How many of them are job-hoppers? In looking at my most successful clients and colleagues, the resounding answer is zero.

But wait a minute, Colleen. You're old school. Times have changed. The new generation is different. Really? Would Mark Zuckerberg have built Facebook if he decided to job-hop two years after starting the company? Do great athletes switch from football to basketball to track and field because they feel a calling to a new career every two years?

Step into your client's shoes. Clients don't enjoy educating and building relationships with a new salesperson every year. Trust and relationships are built over time. Instant gratification salespeople don't put in the time to build deep client relationships.

Are there exceptions to this job-hopping debate? Sure, and one such exception are young sales professionals in their twenties. These individuals often start their careers in an inside sales or business development role, many of which are designed for a two-year stint. If a company doesn't have a career path for young, ambitious sales professionals, they will move to organizations offering a better career path in sales.

Go back to your twenties. You may have changed jobs more in your twenties. It's always been the decade of figuring it out. This isn't new behavior. I had four different jobs in my twenties before I landed in this rewarding career of sales and with a great company where I stayed for ten years.

Vet your new hire for delayed gratification skills. Avoid hiring sales marshmallow grabbers and cookie monsters.

Sales EQ Interview Questions

1. How do you plan your week? (Proactive planning takes time. You have to put in the work to achieve a well-run week.)
2. What is the hardest goal you've worked to achieve? What made it hard? How long did you work to achieve the goal?
3. Describe to me a skill that you've mastered. How did you achieve mastery? How many hours of practice or time did you invest to master it?

4. What is the largest account you've sold? How long did it take? What were some of the obstacles in getting the deal across the line?

5. Give me an example of a time when you gave up on achieving a goal. How long had you pursued the goal?

6. Share with me your pre-call planning strategy when meeting with a new prospect. Or, upselling a new line of business to a client.

7. What are you doing today to make sure your skills and knowledge remain relevant?

Recruit and hire salespeople with delayed gratification skills. Avoid hiring cookie monsters and marshmallow grabbers. You need salespeople who are willing to put in the work to reap the many rewards of masterful sales.

5

Passion, Perseverance, and Sales Performance

A FEW YEARS AGO, I was having a conversation with a successful colleague of mine, who is also in the sales training business. Pete had just returned from an appointment, one where the purpose and objective was to close a $100,000 deal. Upon arriving at the company, his supposed-to-be new client apologized and informed him that the company had made a decision to sell the firm.

I asked, "Ugh . . . what did you do?"

He responded without missing a beat, "Some will, some won't, moving on. In fact, this deal not coming through has actually taught me a few lessons on how to be better in the next selling situation." No time was lost to a pity party or "why me" conversation.

That's resiliency. That's perseverance. That's success.

Now here's the backstory on Pete. He grew up in a home with an alcoholic father. At a very young age, Pete became the provider of the house, both emotionally and financially. If you were going to measure an individual on resiliency and perseverance, my colleague would score off the charts. His not so easy childhood produced a very resilient individual.

And to Pete's credit, he didn't harbor resentment toward a childhood cut short because he also possessed the EQ skill of optimism. More than once, he shared that his tough upbringing was a gift. Those difficult early years gave him the gift of resiliency and perseverance.

So you might be wondering: Should sales managers only hire salespeople who come from broken homes, dysfunctional families, or difficult backgrounds? The answer is no. But what I am suggesting is that sales managers put intense focus on hiring salespeople who possess the muscles of perseverance and resiliency.

These traits are often developed during a person's childhood and are difficult to develop when a person reaches adulthood. Sales leaders don't have the time or expertise to develop these important competencies.

Resiliency and Revenues

Back in 1997, an early pioneer in the study of resiliency, Paul Stoltz, authored the book *Adversity Quotient, Turning Obstacles into Opportunities*. This is a great book where he shares nineteen years of research and ten years of application toward answering the question "Why do some people persist, while others fall short or even quit?"

If you've been in sales leadership long enough, you've probably hired a salesperson who should have been successful and wasn't. The resume looked great. During the interview, the salesperson sounded like a winner. What sales managers often miss in the interview process is vetting the salesperson for their ability to withstand and overcome adversity. Stoltz calls it the Adversity Quotient®.

I've seen salespeople with impressive resumes fail when they move to another sales organization. The new sales environment is more difficult than the salesperson's previous environment. Their new sales position requires more resiliency, more perseverance.

The Need for Resiliency

Years ago, one of my clients hired a salesperson with a strong sales background. She ended up failing miserably. It wasn't due to lack of sales talent; it was lack of resiliency.

At her previous company, the salesperson sold a well-branded product. My client's company didn't have a well-known brand so gaining access to prospects was a lot more difficult. The salesperson's previous stellar track record was based on selling a need-to-have product, one where there was a deadline for renewals and implementation. My client sold high-end management consulting services, a nice-to-have service, but one that is easy for prospects to stall because there isn't a deadline.

The salesperson got frustrated. She wasn't willing to put in the extra work needed to learn how to sell to this new set of buyers and resigned within a year. My client learned that difficult lesson of how previous sales experience doesn't always translate to future sales success. On her next sales hire, she interviewed extensively for resiliency, knowing she needed a salesperson who could and would persevere in spite of setbacks.

Are You Building a Campground or a High-Performance Sales Team?

In his book, Stoltz writes about three types of people: quitters, campers, and climbers. Let's take his descriptions and apply them to the process of hiring great salespeople.

A quitter is a person who resists change. These salespeople wreak havoc on a sales culture because they tend to be frustrated individuals. As a result, they make sure everyone else on the team is equally miserable. These salespeople have given up on their goals and refuse to "climb." Hopefully, these types of individuals don't even make it to the phone screening interview.

Campers, by Stoltz's definition, are individuals who lead compromised lives. At some point, they may have even been climbers but are just tired of the climb. These individuals start camping and settling for "good enough." Their business development efforts are good enough. Their selling skills are good enough. Their sales results are good enough. Sales campers have lost their desire to learn and grow.

These individuals are frustrating to manage because they do just enough to keep their jobs. Campers are salespeople who:

- Almost hit quota, but never quite make it. Sales managers wonder if it's them or the salesperson.
- Show some initiative, some drive, but never enough to make a substantial change in their sales results or your sales organization.
- Take calculated risks. Sales managers teach and coach sales campers how to call on new markets or try new ideas, but their desire for comfort wins. The sales manager keeps talking and the sales campers keep doing what they are doing.

It's easy for sales leaders to hire a sales camper who was once a climber. Their resume is full of previous accomplishments and sales awards. They might be salespeople who have been in the industry a long time. They have a lot of connections and contacts. But many have no desire to learn new selling approaches. They have connections but are really tired of prospecting and business development. They only focus on meeting with existing accounts. A young sales professional can also be a sales camper. They lack the intrinsic motivation to learn and improve. Sales campers are motivated by comfort, not climbing.

Sales managers who make the mistake of hiring sales campers build big sales campgrounds. They are filled with salespeople sitting around the campfire, eating smores and talking about the good old days.

Look for and hire what Stoltz refers to as climbers. These people are passionate about life, continuous learning, and improving. Stoltz's research shows that climbers, in any position, contribute the most to organizations.

Climbers understand adversity is just a part of life. And the profession of sales can present a lot of adversity such as:

- A salesperson has been working on an opportunity for two years and now it's stalled because a new decision maker has joined the prospect's company and is thinking about bringing in his existing supplier.
- A salesperson has one of those months where they hear more noes than yeses.
- The new product launch is failing miserably and 25 percent of the salesperson's goal was based on sales from that line of business.
- Out of the blue, the prospect's budget was cut and so was the salesperson's sale.
- The salesperson won the sale and now discovers the new client is a nightmare client.

Hire salespeople who will persevere, continue climbing, and continue improving. These salespeople are better at handling the obstacles that happen in business and in life.

A Sales Climber

I met Samantha at a networking event. She was young, bright, and a sales climber. As we engaged in conversation, she shared her excitement of starting with a small company that was growing rapidly. "This is a great opportunity for me because I'm new to sales. The only downside is that the CEO, who is also acting as sales manager, is really busy so I don't get a lot of direction." Her eyes narrowed and her smile got even bigger. "But I've figured out a way to get training. He's in the office by 6:30 a.m. every morning. So, twice a week I show up at 7:00 a.m. and ask for fifteen minutes of his time. I'm really organized, have my questions ready, and he gives me a short lesson on sales each time."

That's a sales climber. Think about how easy it would be for this young sales professional to throw in the towel embossed with the words "I quit." Many would simply complain about lack of training and mentoring. Samantha's resiliency and perseverance drove her to overcome obstacles. She set her alarm, got up, got out, and grabbed coaching whenever she could from a very busy executive.

Take a lesson from the great spiritual teacher Buddha. "If you want to draw water, you do not dig six one-foot wells. You dig one six-foot well."

Salespeople who lack perseverance tend to dig a lot of one-foot wells. They are sales campers.

- They practice their selling skills a little—but never enough to become masterful.
- They study product knowledge enough to get them by, not enough to make them a sought-after expert in their industry.

- They do some sales activity but not enough consistent activity to produce a full sales pipeline.

Digging six-foot wells requires perseverance. It requires sales climbers.

Perseverance, Optimism, and Revenues

Optimism is an emotional intelligence skill, one that sometimes creates visions of an over-the-top, glad-handing, not-in-touch-with-reality salesperson. Again, Stein and Book share a better picture of optimism in their book, *The EQ Edge*:

> Optimism isn't about indulging in a perpetual pep talk or simply repeating positive things to yourself. Rather it's the ability to stop thinking or saying destructive things about yourself and the world around you, especially when you're suffering personal setbacks. True optimism is a comprehensive and hopeful but realistic approach to daily living.

This thing called life is full of disappointments, setbacks, and adversity. You'll find that many high performers, including many CEOs, have encountered more than their share of adversity. The difference is always their perspective on adversity. These successful people are sincerely thankful for adversity, saying things like, "It's made me a more empathetic person. I know I can accomplish anything because I was able to push through this setback."

Psychologist Martin Seligman is well known for his work around optimism. In my first book, I shared his research showing that optimistic insurance salespeople outsold their pessimistic peers by 88 percent.

His extensive research shows that optimistic people are better equipped to deal with adversity because they look at life through a different lens. Their lens of the world is that a setback is only temporary and limited. Pessimistic people have a very different lens, viewing setbacks as permanent and pervasive.

Listen to an optimistic and pessimistic salesperson and you will hear a distinct difference in their self-talk, their belief systems. The optimistic salesperson experiencing a sales slump views the slump as temporary, not permanent.

"This is a temporary setback. I've been here before and I know what to do. I've got the ability to get sales back on track."

The pessimistic salesperson caves to a different type of selling behavior and self-talk that the problem is permanent and pervasive.

"There's nothing I can do about this situation. None of my prospects are buying right now. This economy is never going to get better."

Salespeople with low optimism lack the ability to quickly get back in the sales saddle when disappointment hits. They lose weeks of productivity because they don't have the "bounce-back factor." Think of a quarterback taking a long break after getting sacked or throwing an interception. Not happening! Sales organizations lose thousands of dollars every year because they hire salespeople who can't get back up after being "sacked" or throw the sales ball again after experiencing a difficult sales meeting.

Look for and hire optimistic salespeople. They are easy to recognize as they are the ones running around with glasses that are always full, not half empty.

Where Is Your Potential Sales Candidate's Focus?

I am all about making a sales manager's life easier. And life becomes much easier when sales managers hire salespeople with a high internal locus of control. It's been described as an individual's belief that success in life is attributed to his or her own efforts rather than external circumstances.

Back in the 1950s, American psychologist Julian Rotter conducted research showing that people with a high internal locus of control believe they can control their outcomes, despite external factors. Since that early research, other studies show that individuals with a high internal locus of control produce more work and better work. They also enjoy a higher degree of career satisfaction. This is a winning formula for hiring great salespeople.

The salesperson with an internal locus of control looks inward for answers and solutions. If the company isn't generating enough leads, they take charge and figure out ways to fill their sales pipeline. If the company doesn't have certain systems and processes in place, they install their own systems and processes in order to get the job done.

The salesperson with an external locus of control is an expert at the blame game. He is great at finding—and blaming—external forces for his lack of success. This salesperson possesses a victim mentality, believing that life is happening to him. Therefore, he's not responsible for his outcomes or actions. In the world of psychology, this is defined as learned helplessness. It's the internal belief that what you do does not matter. This belief quickly saps a person's sense of control and ownership.

These salespeople are exhausting to manage. External locus of control salespeople are masters at turning their sales manager into an act at the circus. Has anyone had a ringside seat at this show? The sales manager keeps jumping through hoops, trying to meet the demands for more "external" resources from her salesperson. As she jumps through one hoop and then another, the salesperson demands still more resources. This circus act never stops because this type of salesperson never takes responsibility for her own success.

Your job as a sales manager is to identify and disqualify these salespeople *quickly*. They are actually not that hard to spot because an external locus of control salesperson has always had a history of blame (see Figure 5.1).

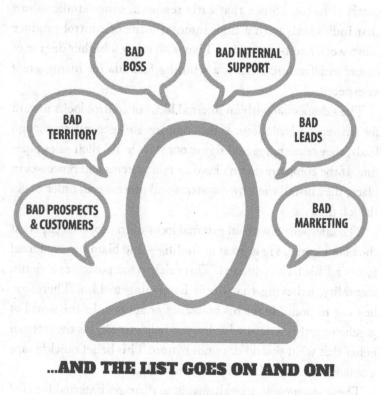

BAD
BOSS

BAD INTERNAL
SUPPORT

BAD
TERRITORY

BAD
LEADS

BAD PROSPECTS
& CUSTOMERS

BAD
MARKETING

...AND THE LIST GOES ON AND ON!

FIGURE 5.1

But take a closer look—the common denominator is them!

I fully support trying to remove obstacles and providing resources for salespeople to be successful. But in life and business, there are always going to be obstacles and lack of resources, especially in fast-growth sales organizations. I know because I started in sales with a fast-growth company. When companies are growing, there will be times when internal systems, processes, and resources just can't keep up. Resilient salespeople figure it out. They have the ability to push through the tough times, push through adversity.

A Lesson in Sales Resiliency

Angie Stevens and I worked together at Varsity. Today, they are the largest company in the world in their industry. They've done many things well and one is hiring people with a high internal locus of control. Angie Stevens is one of those individuals. In the early years at Varsity, it was difficult to forecast production of camp wear. For those of you not familiar with the cheerleading business, this is the matching sportswear that cheerleaders wear to camp each day.

In the fashion business, it's difficult to predict which design is going to sell. When I was a sportswear buyer in my twenties, we were always trying to forecast "what piece of merchandise was going to blow out of the store."

More than once at Varsity, we'd have a sleeper design that would start "blowing out of the warehouse." It was stressful managing the unexpected influx of orders.

As vice president of sales, I observed two distinct responses from my sales team in dealing with this challenge. The first response was high locus of control. Instead of complaining about the situation, these salespeople focused on taking control of the situation. The second response was, as you probably have already guessed, a low internal locus of control. These salespeople would sit back and complain loudly about the situation.

Angie Stevens was in the first bucket. She was very proactive about follow-up, calling her customers two weeks ahead of camp dates to double-check deliveries. When working with her coaches and customers, she was very diligent about uncovering the dates they planned to attend cheer camp.

The external locus of control reps (thankfully we didn't have that many) favored another approach. Their responses included, "That's not my job. This is the production department's problem. I sold it—they need to get the merchandise delivered." Their external locus of control, not taking responsibility, created a lot of unnecessary firefighting.

Angie ignored that type of self-talk and approach. She may not have been able to control production; however, she knew she could control giving herself enough time to get another solution in place. It's no wonder she was consistently one of the top reps in the company.

Take a look at this chart and ask yourself what type of salespeople you've been hiring.

Internal Locus of Control Salesperson	External Locus of Control Salesperson
Looks inward for answers *and* solutions.	Looks outward for answers *and* solutions. Waits to be rescued.
Focuses on resources she has. Finds and creates new resources.	Complains about lack of resources. Waits for someone else to find and provide.
Takes 100 percent responsibility for sales success.	Blames external factors for lack of sales success.
Asks the question: What can I do to change my circumstances to be more successful?	Asks the question: What circumstances need to change in order for me to be successful?

Will You Persevere?

Building a great sales team starts with you. Apply self-awareness and examine your sales management behaviors. Have you invested the time in learning and mastering behavior-based interview questions? Do you have weekly or monthly goals for interviewing top sales talent, even when you don't have an open position? Are you digging a one-foot well or a six-foot well?

Hiring great salespeople is difficult for several reasons. The first is that people often get into sales as a default profession. "I'm going to do this until I find something better." Twenty years later, they still haven't found something better. They retire while working on the job.

Sales managers and CEOs have new challenges in recruiting and hiring today because of changing dynamics in the family unit and technology. Let me explain.

The boomers are retiring and young sales professionals are taking their place. Many boomers grew up in large families with five to ten kids. The sheer size of the families often created more resilient people. It wasn't anything special the parents were doing. It's called survival. Parents simply couldn't do everything themselves. I grew up in a family with eight children. My parents ran a small office that never closed! (And they couldn't fire any of the employees—we had immediate tenure.) Everyone was assigned chores at a young age in order to keep the "office" running. It didn't matter if you were young or tired. The work had to get done. This environment created resiliency, responsibility, and accountability.

Technology is also a contributor in creating less resilient individuals. Again, "back in the day" a person just didn't pick up the phone and call their parents for advice. Long-distance calls were very expensive. There were no cell phones, so access to adults and advice wasn't easy. This non-tech environment forced people to make decisions and live with the consequences of those decisions.

Today, parents are dispensing advice all day long through phone or text. Many young people aren't learning how to think through their own challenges or deal with adversity.

I'm not jumping on the popular bandwagon bashing young sales professionals. I'm actually tired of the hit tune named, "Young people are lazy and entitled." Believe me, I've met my share of lazy, entitled boomers. But the reality is that sales managers are faced with different challenges in hiring as they have more sales candidates who are products of helicopter parenting and technology.

Don't settle! Persevere in your search for the right salespeople. Not every sales candidate grew up on a street named easy.

Sales managers may need to look longer and further, but good salespeople of all ages are out there. I have worked with sales rock stars in all age groups. Make sure you aren't camping, settling, and looking for an easy path to hiring great salespeople. There isn't one or we would all be on it!

Sales Universities

Many of my clients are partnering with the progressive universities that offer sales degrees. This is great news for sales managers because these graduates aren't defaulting to the profession of sales. They have chosen sales and have a passion for sales. They recognize sales as a great career path for individuals who want to be rewarded for perseverance and personal performance.

Sales managers, apply delayed gratification and put in the work to establish relationships with local and national universities. Recruit early and often in a young professional's life. Keep your people pipeline full.

Winning the Future

One of my clients, Gallagher, is a great example of partnering with colleges to build their sales force of the future. The company has developed an incredible intern program that attracts over four hundred new, young recruits annually. The company hires many of them upon college graduation, approximately 60 percent.

What's equally impressive is the amount of training and mentoring they provide for their new recruits. Each new hire is enrolled in a two-year program where they learn skills on emotional intelligence, networking, prospecting, sales, and product knowledge. Senior executives at Gallagher take time out of their busy schedules and get involved in judging the sales contests. They host networking events where the senior executives meet the new hires, providing great insights and support. This company attracts top sales talent because they persevere in their goal of hiring the best and the brightest.

Test your sales candidates for the competencies of adversity, resilience, and perseverance. Find out if your candidate is willing to do their "first year."

Sales EQ Interview Questions

1. Tell me about the hardest you've ever worked to achieve a goal. (Test for perseverance.)
2. Why have you switched jobs every two years?
   (Hint: Job-hoppers often lack the perseverance it takes to succeed. When the going gets tough—they get going.)

3. Share with me the biggest adversity you've faced in your life. What did you do to overcome it? (Has your candidate ever faced obstacles?)

4. What are some of the biggest decisions you've had to make on your own? (Is this candidate going to need their parent with them on a sales call?)

5. Tell me about a time when you wanted to give up but you didn't. What made you keep going? (Will this candidate dig a one-foot well or a six-foot well?)

6. What have you done to prevent a potential problem in the delivery of your products or services? (Check for internal or external locus of control.)

7. Tell me about a time you took responsibility for fixing a problem you didn't create. (Internal locus of control people take charge and deliver results.)

Sales is a great profession, one that requires the ability to persevere and push through adversity. Hire salespeople who aren't looking for greener pastures. Hire salespeople who *make* greener pastures.

6

Assertiveness
and
Sales Results

I WAS WITH A group of colleagues and we were sharing stories of our first jobs. One of our successful colleagues had us howling as he told us his adventures in his first job as a paperboy. He grew up in a lower-middle-class neighborhood so let's just say some of his customers could be a little difficult.

He would wake up at 4:00 a.m., load up his bike with papers, and work like crazy to deliver them before the 7:00 a.m. deadline. Only if the weather was really bad would he wake up his father to help finish the job.

The real fun began after school, when he'd start collecting money from his customers. Many of them had already had a cocktail by 4:00 p.m. so they enjoyed "messing" with a ten-year-old, saying they weren't going to pay. Many attempted to shortchange him, pretending to give him ten dollars when in reality they'd only given him five dollars. Customers shut doors in his face, telling him to come back later—like in twenty years.

But my colleague, even at the age of ten, was assertive. He possessed the ability to state what he needed, even when doing so was emotionally difficult. He'd continue to knock on closed doors, stand his ground with customers twice his size, and collect his hard-earned money. His assertiveness has served him well in his career as a top sales professional. He's exceptionally good at asking for what he needs during the sales process.

Assertiveness Is Not a Behavioral Style

Assertive salespeople are able to stand up for what they need and do it in a way that doesn't offend other people. Sales managers not interviewing for this skill run the chance of hiring a salesperson who is passive-aggressive. These salespeople have a high need for approval and a need to go-along-to-get-along. These go-along-to-get-along salespeople avoid holding the difficult conversations that are inherently part of life, sales, and business. For example, a client requests a scope change in a project, however, doesn't want to pay additional fees. The passive-aggressive salesperson avoids the assertive conversation that needs to happen, doesn't charge the client, and the project profitability decreases. Not because of mistakes or missed deadlines. Because the salesperson lacked the assertiveness to state what was needed: payment for a requested scope change.

Interviewing for assertiveness often gets missed in the interview process. The pre-hire assessment shows that your potential candidate is a high driver, dominant, and results-oriented salesperson. We immediately conclude this salesperson is assertive. Be careful. Don't confuse a behavioral style with an emotional intelligence skill.

Assertiveness Can Be Learned

Jennifer was a classic example of a high driver who needed more development with her assertiveness. She was really good at the discovery step, controlling her impulse to immediately offer advice. Jennifer had great problem-solving skills, which helped potential clients understand the impact of doing nothing. Then, she'd blow it during the budget stage of the sales process. When asking the prospect for the investment they'd set aside to purchase her digital marketing services, the prospect would give the typical answer, "I don't know . . . we've never invested in this before . . . just put something together."

Jennifer's assertiveness would go right out the window and she'd go-along-to-get-along. She would write a recommendation without uncovering if the prospect was willing or able to invest in her services. Valuable time was invested in writing more than one proposal for unqualified prospects. "This is more than I wanted to invest. We'll need to delay this decision."

Chalk up another practice proposal to lack of assertiveness.

The good news is Jennifer is self-aware and humble and invested in coaching. In fact, I'll never forget one rather tough-love coaching session. She was giving me several yeah-but-you-don't-understand excuses. "Yeah, but the prospect really doesn't have a budget. Yeah, but they've never invested in digital marketing before so they don't know what to invest."

I shared the same advice I received from an early mentor when I was hearing similar answers from my prospects. He calmly stated, "If your prospect doesn't have a budget, how can he tell you that your price is too high? Your prospect has a budget. Let's discuss how your lack of assertiveness is affecting your ability to uncover that budget."

How and Where Low Assertiveness Affects Sales Results

Hire a salesperson who lacks assertiveness and you will see the impact on sales results in various selling steps and stages. Let's look at three other areas where lack of assertiveness affects the accuracy of sales forecasts and achievement of sales goals.

Decision Step

Salespeople lacking assertiveness have difficulty gaining access to the right decision maker or all of the buying influences. It's not because the salesperson lacks knowledge. The sales manager has taught them the Sales IQ skills, the consultative selling skills, needed to gain access to all the buying influences. Tactics such as:

"Mr. Buyer. I think we've had a good conversation today and I do believe my company can help with some of your challenges and goals. However, where we've had the best success is when we also meet with your chief marketing officer. Can you help me get that meeting set up?"

That's an easy enough request, right? Not for the nonassertive salesperson. They know they should ask the question but avoid asking the question for fear of not being liked or rocking the sales boat. They go-along-to-get-along and the request is never stated. Your company loses to a more assertive salesperson, one who asked to get a meeting with other decision makers.

Big Sales Pipelines Full of Unqualified Prospects

Meet nonassertive Henry. He is conducting a first meeting with a prospect and it's one of those nice sales meetings. You know, those meetings where the prospect says all the right things. "We think it's a good idea to look every few years. We've heard good things about your organization." But with closer analysis, there really is no compelling reason for this prospect to change and invest in your services.

The prospect asks Henry to put together a recommendation. Now, nonassertive Henry recognizes there is no pain to solve or goal to achieve. However, he lacks the assertiveness to state the obvious and goes-along-to-get-along. He invests hours writing a recommendation only to hear, "This looks really great. The timing isn't quite right . . . can you follow up in ten years?"

Sales managers who hire nonassertive salespeople end up managing sales pipelines that are bursting full—of unqualified prospects. Nonassertive salespeople suffer from carpal tunnel because they write a lot of recommendations for prospects that are never going to buy! They keep prospects in the sales funnel that should have been moved out months ago. It's as if they adopt these prospects—like a pet—because they lack the assertiveness to nicely disqualify them and find them a new home in some other salesperson's pipeline.

> **Lack of assertiveness = practice proposals =
> missed sales forecasts**

Hire an assertive salesperson and the conversation is going to sound a little different. This salesperson is comfortable applying your training and nicely declines to take a next step. "Ms. Prospect, thank you for asking for a recommendation from us. However, based on our conversation today, I don't know if I'm hearing enough reasons for you to change or invest. What am I missing?"

The assertive salesperson states what she needs nicely and what she needs is a qualified opportunity, one where the prospect has a compelling business reason to change, grow, and invest. She doesn't need more practice writing proposals!

Clear Next Steps

Here's another crazy place where low assertiveness shows up during the sales process. Setting clear next steps with a prospect . . . or not. This selling step is so simple. Every good sales trainer, sales manager, and sales coach teaches this concept.

Yet, we've all seen salespeople end a sales meeting or send off a proposal with no date on the calendar to connect or review. It's the sales kiss of death and the beginning of chase mode. Your nonassertive salesperson turns into a sales stalker, one who keeps sending emails and leaving voicemails in hopes of getting a response.

Hire an assertive salesperson and you will find a salesperson who is comfortable stating what she needs. And what she needs is a mutually agreed-upon next step, one that is on both parties' calendars.

The Aggressive Salesperson

A sales manager not vetting a candidate for assertiveness might end up with the opposite communication style and hire an overly aggressive salesperson. This salesperson has no problem stating what he needs except he doesn't know how to ask for what he needs in a manner that doesn't emotionally trigger prospects and customers.

Aggressive selling behaviors result in perfectly qualified prospects choosing to do business with your competitor because aggressive salespeople are often not likeable salespeople. The only way they know how to get results is through pushing or demanding. They might engage in the following nonproductive selling behaviors.

- The aggressive salesperson is too direct, creating a fight-or-flight response in the prospects. The conversation shuts down as does the opportunity.

- The aggressive salesperson asks weird, leading questions, ones that make prospects feel like they are being backed into a corner. "Wouldn't you agree?" Or, "But I thought you said you wanted to eliminate this challenge . . . so, you are okay with the status quo?" Yeah, this is a fun call for your prospect.
- The aggressive salesperson pushes through objections rather than trying to understand objections. Aggressive salespeople talk too much and listen too little. Enough said.

Hire an aggressive salesperson and you will find yourself losing sales because prospects still like to buy from people they like.

Have I Confused You?

If you've been in sales management long enough, you've probably managed a salesperson that has demonstrated all three types of behaviors: assertive, passive-aggressive, and aggressive. It's because the demonstration of emotional intelligence skills is situational. In certain situations, and with certain buyers, a salesperson demonstrates the right amount of assertiveness during the sales conversation. And yet, in other selling scenarios, one of their evil twins takes over the sales call.

A salesperson might default to passive-aggressive behaviors based on their comfort level with the size of the opportunity. When the deal size gets bigger, the salesperson goes along to get along and doesn't ask for what she needs to create a successful partnership.

I've worked with salespeople who are really likeable. And yet, when meeting with certain personality styles, they get emotionally triggered. Out of the blue, their aggressive Attila the Hun personality takes over the sales call. No likeability or sale.

Do you hire or not hire a salesperson who does not have the skill of assertiveness fully developed? The answer is yes and no. Evaluate other soft skills in the interview process such as the salesperson's self-awareness and willingness to be coached. Emotional intelligence skills can be improved and the coachable salesperson is happy to hear and apply feedback.

Analyze how much time it will take for you to help your potential new hire to develop this skill. Do you have the time to invest? Is this "something" you are willing to live with or is this pebble going to become a rock?

Sales managers, take a look at your assertiveness during the interviewing process. Observe your own style and determine if you are going-along-to-get-along when interviewing candidates. Maybe you avoid asking the tougher questions, deeper questions, or simply more questions.

Be assertive in your interview process and ask the assertive questions to determine if this candidate should be on your sales bus.

Sales EQ Interview Questions

1. Tell me about a sales call where the prospect was hesitant to share their budget or didn't have a budget. What did you do? What was the outcome?
2. Give me an example of a time when a prospect didn't want to introduce you to other decision makers in the organization. What did you say and do?
3. Share a time where you disqualified an opportunity because the prospect wasn't a good fit for your company. What did you say and do when the prospect asked you for a proposal after you decided to disqualify them?

4. Give me an example of a sales call where the prospect wasn't willing to set up clear next steps after a meeting. What did you say and do?

5. Tell me about a time when you had to challenge a prospect on their current approach, product, or solution. What questions did you ask? What was the outcome of the conversation?

Assertive salespeople are comfortable stating what they need to create true win-win partnerships. And they state what they need in a way that doesn't emotionally trigger prospects or customers. Avoid hiring passive-aggressive or aggressive salespeople to avoid missed sales forecasts.

7

Are You Hiring a Learner or a Laggard?

RESEARCH CONDUCTED BY TOM Corley, author of *Rich Habits*, found that 88 percent of wealthy people read thirty minutes for self-improvement each day as compared to 2 percent of the non-wealthy. He also found that only 6 percent of the wealthy watch reality TV versus 78 percent of the non-wealthy. Goodbye, Kardashians!

In an interview with Oprah Winfrey, Tony Robbins, the megasuccessful life coach, shared his rags-to-riches story. He was kicked out of the house at seventeen and decided the only way up and out was to gain knowledge. He took a speed-reading course and read seven hundred books in seven years. I think it's safe to assume that his thirst for learning helped him build a multimillion-dollar speaking and training empire.

Warren Buffet, founder of Berkshire Hathaway, was asked how to get smarter. He held up stacks of paper and said, "Read five hundred pages like this every day. That's how knowledge builds up, like compound interest." Now, I've had more than one salesperson push back when hearing Mr. Buffet's advice. "Well, he's a billionaire. He has time to read." My not so EQ, very direct response is, "Maybe he's a billionaire because he takes time to read, study, and improve."

Michael Simmons, founder of Empact, coined the *five-hour rule*. The concept is pretty simple. No matter how busy successful people are, they always spend at least an hour a day—or five hours a week—learning or practicing. And they do this across their entire career.

A Learning Sales Culture

My personal experience in working with highly successful CEOs, sales managers, and salespeople is they share a common trait of continuous improvement or self-actualization. According to American psychologist Abraham Maslow, self-actualization represents growth of an individual toward fulfillment of the highest needs, and in particular, a meaning in life.

A desire to learn and grow is one of the main psychographics we look for when meeting with prospects. Without this attribute, training and development gets put in the expense line of the company budget rather than the investment line of the budget. We only get hired by companies that believe that continuous improvement leads to sustainable sales success.

Many of our clients belong to peer advisory groups such as Vistage, TAB, Chief Executive Network, or Young Presidents' Organization. These busy executives don't have more time than other executives: They make time to remain relevant. They make time to learn.

It may just be a coincidence, but our clients who have built true learning organizations continue to hit sales targets year after year.

The ROI of a Learning Sales Organization

Eric Amhaus is a learner and vice president of sales at Pie Consulting and Engineering. They've experienced 189 percent growth in revenues over the last five years. This company doesn't just talk about development, they do development, investing time and money in their people. In a two-year period, they invested $657,757 and over 36,000 hours in various training and coaching programs ranging from hiring to leadership to sales to technical training. They also have a number of internal training programs, which include a well-defined ninety-day onboarding program, a customized sales playbook, annual goal development plans, monthly one-on-one meetings for every employee with managers, and annual retreats. Pie believes in sharing the fruits of their success. Their staff donated over 775 hours back to the community. I wonder if any of their success can be attributed to a learning culture?

The Disconnect

When I speak to CEO groups or sales management groups, I ask participants to share specific questions they incorporate in their interview process to determine their potential sales candidate's appetite and aptitude for learning. The request is met with blank stares followed by a mumbled, "Uh, we don't."

No wonder CEOs and sales leaders are frustrated. They keep investing time and money in training and coaching salespeople who don't have the ability or desire to learn.

Let me be really blunt.

If you hire a salesperson who doesn't value learning, the longer this individual works for you, the dumber this person will be.

My husband, Jim, is an attorney. Each year he attends courses to earn his continuing education "CLEs" in order to keep his license. When he turned sixty-five, he received a notice saying he no longer had to attend these courses. He thought the notice was hysterical. "Oh, so now that I'm sixty-five, I get to be a dumb lawyer." (In Colorado, they have since changed the rule.)

Unfortunately, sales managers hire a lot of salespeople who don't believe they need to earn sales CLEs every year. It's that attitude that breeds arrogance and mediocrity. Know-it-all thinking leads to complacency, which results in losing business to a competitor that is constantly studying, learning, and improving.

Valued Partner or Transactional Salesperson

Sales gurus preach the value of a salesperson being a value-added partner to clients. Sales managers teach the importance of being a trusted advisor to clients, a person who offers insights and thought leadership to clients.

Blah, blah, blah.

A salesperson can't be a trusted advisor or thought leader if she isn't learning any new thoughts! Without the desire to learn, a salesperson ends up working with the same set of data that made her successful ten years ago. She is a VCR player in a streaming video world.

Hiring salespeople who have the ability and desire to learn is no longer a luxury or option to be successful in sales. It is critical to remain relevant and competitive.

Take a look at your industry. Have you experienced significant changes in how you do business in the last six months? One year? Two years? The answer is yes and the pace of change is not letting up. Between 600,000 and 1,000,000 books are published each year. In the last two years alone, 90 percent of the data in the world was generated. Remaining relevant is a competitive edge, one that requires hiring salespeople who have a desire and discipline to keep learning and improving.

Hire the Buggers of the World

Angela Duckworth is the author of *Grit: The Power of Passion and Perseverance*. Her research shows that highly accomplished people are paragons of perseverance. The underlying reason for their perseverance is passion. Put these two traits together and you will find that highly accomplished salespeople are passionate about what they are trying to learn or master.

Passionate salespeople persevere in their personal development. They don't wait for the company to make them good; they recognize it's their responsibility to become the best. I call these salespeople the "buggers" of the world.

- They bug their sales managers for coaching.
- They bug senior sales representatives for information and advice.
- They bug their peers to engage in more role-plays.

If you want to achieve sales goals year after year, hire the "buggers" of the world. One of my successful sales executives, Sam Winfrey, shared his strategy for becoming a top sales producer:

> In my early years, I knew I wasn't that good; [self-awareness] however, I knew someone at my company was. I quickly figured out who the top salespeople were and offered to buy them lunch. People have to eat so while these top sales producers were eating, I'd ask all sorts of questions around sales, product, and service.

Sam is a bugger. He was and still is passionate about learning. He persevered in garnering coaching time with veterans who didn't have time to spare.

Make sure your next sales hire is a person who has the aptitude and attitude needed for continuous improvement. It's a competitive business environment. Prospects and customers want to work with salespeople who make their brains hurt and help them see new ways of looking at their own business. The learners of the world are the trusted advisors of the world.

Sales EQ Interview Questions

1. Give me an example of a new skill you had to learn in your previous jobs. How did you go about learning the new skill? How did you know you had mastered the new skill?
2. In the past, what have you done to remain relevant in industry knowledge?
3. Tell me about the three best sales/business books you've read or listened to. What did you apply from these books and how did the information help you win more business?
4. Share with me what you are currently learning to provide value to your clients.
5. Tell me how you incorporate continuous learning into your busy schedule.
6. Give me an example of when you've invested in your own learning. How about training?
7. What mentors have you sought out to improve your understanding of business?

Hire salespeople who are motivated to keep changing, learning, growing, and improving. Hire learners, not laggards.

8

Is Your New Sales Hire Coachable?

DR. EVE GRODNITZKY IS a research psychologist and works with organizations all over the world. I had the good fortune of hearing her speak. During her presentation, she asked the audience a provocative question around hiring.

"Are you in the behavior-modification business or in the behavior-selection business?"

That's a great question. Sales leaders often get stuck in the role of psychologist and psychotherapist because they didn't hire coachable salespeople, individuals who are comfortable with performance feedback.

Have you ever noticed that everyone says they want feedback—until they receive it? I've observed more than one CEO and sales manager waste valuable time and energy trying to coach a non-coachable salesperson. This type of salesperson has a high need to be right, difficulty admitting mistakes, and gets defensive when receiving well-intended feedback.

Managing a non-coachable salesperson is exhausting. And unfortunately, many sales managers give in to exhaustion and stop giving feedback. They slowly allow unacceptable selling behaviors and attitudes to creep into their sales culture, creating status quo and mediocre sales teams. Non-coachable salespeople cost sales organizations thousands of dollars.

The Corporate Executive Board conducted a study showing that companies that fostered honest and open feedback produced a return over a ten-year period that was 270 percent higher than those that didn't. That number should motivate all of us to get serious about hiring coachable salespeople, ones who seek out feedback rather than push back on feedback.

In my years of working with hundreds of sales organizations, I have found important emotional intelligence skills to look for in the interview process to determine if your sales candidate is coachable.

#1. Self-Regard and Self-Esteem

In the emotional intelligence world, this is defined as "an inner confidence." A salesperson with true confidence has the ability to accept and admit strengths and weaknesses. These individuals refuse to participate in the blame game. They're responsible and accountable for their actions and outcomes.

Sales organizations employing high self-regard individuals move fast because these are "raise your hand" cultures. Confident salespeople raise their hand, admit mistakes, and ask for advice on how to prevent or solve problems. CEOs and sales managers can immediately focus time and energy on improving a situation rather than scrambling to find a solution because they discovered a problem too late.

Adrian Gostick and Chester Elton, authors of *The Orange Revolution, How One Great Team Can Transform an Entire Organization*, share a great example in their book about the power of "raise your hand" cultures. They interviewed Scott Beare, a pilot who flew with the elite Blue Angels flying unit. Scott explained that after the live demonstration of daring maneuvers, the entire group of pilots got together to debrief. They went over every mistake and miscommunication in an environment of total honesty. Here's what really caught my attention. Beare said, "If I was flying too low or a half-second off my mark, either I tell the group or they tell me."

That is a coachable culture. You have some of the most talented pilots in the world who are open to admitting mistakes and learning. They don't hide mistakes or wait for someone to discover errors. They raise their hands.

Patty McCord, author of *Powerful: Building a Culture of Freedom and Responsibility*, shares stories of her fourteen years at Netflix as chief talent officer. Patty said that open sharing of criticism was one of the hardest parts of the Netflix culture for new employees to get used to. Patty calls it radical honesty. Netflix continues to grow at an astonishing rate and I contend one of the reasons is because of their culture of feedback, coachability, and making necessary changes quickly.

#2. A Growth Mindset

Carol Dweck is the author of *Mindset: Changing the Way You Think to Fulfill Your Potential.* In her groundbreaking research, Dweck shared the difference between people with a fixed mindset and a growth mindset. People with a growth mindset believe they can learn and change. These individuals welcome feedback because they see it as a necessary tool to continue on their path of personal and professional improvement. They are coachable.

Avoid hiring the fixed mindset salesperson. As you might have already concluded, this salesperson exhibits the opposite traits. They are not used to failing (or admitting they've failed) so they avoid challenges. These individuals spend most of their time *confirming* their intelligence rather than *improving* their intelligence. Their focus is on making sure you know how smart they are, which limits their desire (or ability) to ask for coaching. The smartest people in the room quickly become the dumbest people in the room.

#3. Humble and Coachable

I've found that the most successful sales leaders are humble leaders. You're probably one of those sales leaders because you've picked up yet another book to learn how to be better, do better. Humble sales leaders don't subscribe to their own press releases. They give credit to others easily and limit the attention directed toward their accomplishments. Humble sales leaders are great team players and build great sales teams.

But here is where I see a big disconnect in sales organizations. Humble sales leaders seem to think it's okay to hire self-absorbed, arrogant salespeople. I've heard more than one CEO and sales manager state that top salespeople are high-maintenance prima donnas. "It just goes with the territory."

I am going to vehemently challenge that belief. Do self-absorbed, arrogant salespeople build great sales cultures? Will high-maintenance salespeople create a work environment where other people want to show up to work every day? No and no.

CEOs and sales managers recognize and preach the importance of team. They list core values on the website or on office walls. Unfortunately, the message on the website or office walls never hits the halls because companies don't test and interview potential sales candidates for humility. This results in hiring arrogant, non-coachable salespeople who wreak havoc on the sales culture.

Hogan Assessments, a leading maker of workplace personality tests, is launching a new twenty-item scale designed to measure humility in job seekers and leaders. In an interview with *The Wall*

Street Journal, Dr. Sherman, chief science officer for the company, shared, "Most of the thinking suggests leaders should be charismatic, attention-seeking, and persuasive. Yet, such leaders tend to ruin their companies because they take on more than they can handle, are overconfident, and don't listen to feedback from others."

Hmmm, sounds like a common problem that also occurs in hiring salespeople.

Here's another great reason to test and interview your candidate for humility. Every sales consultant, sales speaker, and trainer teaches the importance of active listening. But deep listening requires humility. Arrogant salespeople think they know everything so they don't listen to anything!

Humble salespeople are open to learning from peers and customers. They have a willingness to hear diverse views and suggestions. This openness leads to innovative thinking, disruptive thinking, and thought leadership thinking. Humility drives revenues.

A Little Humble Pie
Goes a Long Way

Many years ago, I was working with a business owner and he shared with me a recent misfire on a new salesperson. The salesperson was smart and hardworking. The resume was a solid track record of year over year success. She had earned all the award trips and clubs. His business was a new industry for the salesperson, which required learning new selling skills and approaches to winning the right type of business.

During the first one-on-one coaching session, the owner sat down to give the salesperson feedback and advice on a couple of deals that didn't close. He was patient, knowing that the losses were due to lack of experience in the industry. He quickly learned his new hire was lousy at receiving feedback. The approach didn't seem to make a difference. The business owner tried the "sandwich method." You know, the approach of sharing something positive, an area of improvement, and wrapping up the conversation with something positive. He quickly discovered his new hire didn't like sandwiches of any sorts. She would immediately place the blame on the business owner for her lack of success. Or respond with each piece of advice given with, "Yeah, but . . ."

My client quickly realized he lacked the time—and therapy skills—to develop this salesperson. I was not involved in the hiring process so I asked my client what he missed in the hiring process. "I ignored my gut. There were red flags that told me that this salesperson was a little arrogant. I chalked up the arrogance to youthfulness when in reality it was a serious character flaw."

Emotionally intelligent sales teams are humble teams and competitive teams. And don't think you can't have both qualities, because we work with these types of sales organizations every day. We disqualify arrogant companies and people because we can't teach them anything!

Go back to chapter three. Every candidate you hire has their "something." When interviewing, get very clear on your nonnegotiables and what you are willing or not willing to accept. Ask the really tough question. Is this candidate coachable?

Sales EQ Interview Questions

1. Tell me about a time when you really screwed up. What did you learn? How did you apply the lesson learned moving forward? (Confident and humble salespeople have plenty of stories to share.)
2. What do you attribute your success to? (Listen to see if they give credit to mentors, peers, parents, or colleagues—or if they attribute all success to themselves.)
3. Share with me your biggest weakness. (Listen to see if the candidate gives you an arrogant answer, one that actually positions their biggest weakness as a strength. "I'm just too organized.")
4. Give me an example of the toughest feedback you've ever received. What did you learn? How did you apply? (You are looking for past experience of this person receiving criticism. Did they deny the feedback or do something positive with it?)
5. Tell me about a time when you proactively sought out feedback or coaching. (Confident and humble people seek out feedback—they don't just wait for it.)

Make your life easier as a CEO, sales manager, or business owner. You didn't sign up to be a psychotherapist; you signed up to be a sales leader. Hire salespeople with self-regard, self-esteem, humility, and a growth mindset. Hire salespeople who value coaching and feedback because it is the breakfast of sales champions.

9

Necessary Endings

I WAS HAVING A conversation with a hyper-responsible, super-accountable VP of sales, whom I will call Victoria. One of the reasons this sales manager is so successful is because she is a non-excuse maker. If she makes a mistake, she owns up to it quickly and doesn't assign blame to other people or departments.

During our coaching session, I was listening to Victoria take responsibility for a salesperson's poor performance. "I haven't given her enough training. We are trying to break into a new market segment and that takes time. We really need to provide more leads to our reps."

I listened patiently and then asked a few pointed questions to raise this sales leader's self-awareness.

"How much sales training did you receive as a salesperson?"
- "Uh . . . little or none. I took charge of my own learning."

"How long did it take you to build your territory or account base?"
- "Not long, because I was working straight commission. I worked like crazy to make it happen."

"How many leads were you given when you started in sales?"
- "None. It was up to me to generate my own leads."

I could see the light bulb turning on above this sales manager's head. She was starting to realize that she was more committed to success than her salesperson. Unfortunately, she had hired a salesperson who was going to find an excuse for lack of sales, regardless of the resources provided.

Sales leaders, this next statement might surprise you. Stop being so responsible and accountable. Because of these wonderful attributes, you might be falling into the trap of being more committed to success than your salesperson.

Like a good poker player, you have to know when to hold 'em and when to fold 'em.

Is it time to fold on a few members of your sales team? There will be times, even with all the right hiring practices and tools, where you still hire a sales dud. It's discouraging because of the work you put into hiring, onboarding, training, and coaching. You're an optimistic person so you keep thinking, "If I just do this . . . maybe if I try this . . ."

Stop. Time to fold 'em.

When conducting our sales management courses, I ask sales managers and CEOs, "How many of you have held onto poor performers for too long?" Almost 100 percent of the participants raise their hands!

In fact, some managers raise both hands!

Let's take a closer look at what makes hard-charging, hard-working CEOs and sales managers hang on to poor performers for too long. There are several reasons but let's review the top three I've observed over the years.

Is Your Salespeople Pipeline Full?

Sales managers teach their sales teams the tactics and strategies to build full sales pipelines. We know that a full sales pipeline sets salespeople free because a salesperson with a full pipeline is free to better disqualify opportunities that aren't a good fit. He isn't doing the desperation dance.

Apply the same advice you give to your sales team. Prospect consistently and build your people pipeline. Full people pipelines set *you* free. Think about it. How many of you would put up with poor selling behaviors and bad attitudes if you had a bench full of qualified salespeople?

You don't have a people problem; you have a recruiting problem. The reason sales managers hang onto poor performers is because they're desperate. They need a warm body to fill a seat, answer the phone, or send an email.

You're desperate because you aren't prospecting each week or each month for top sales talent. When a position opens up, you have limited candidates from whom to choose and end up settling for B and C players rather than A players.

Practice what you preach and prospect for top sales talent consistently.

Did You Hire a Worker?

My late father was an Iowa farmer and he was engaged in some type of farming right up until he died. He had a remarkable work ethic. He remarried in his early seventies and I was happy to hear the news. I gave him a call of congratulations and asked a little bit more about his soon-to-be wife, Mary, as I'd only met her once. I was expecting to hear about their common interests and likes. I still laugh at his answer. "Well, she's a worker!" Keep in mind that his fiancée was also in her seventies. My father's response pretty much sums up the work ethic in my family. We are workers!

If you're wondering whether or not to keep a salesperson on your sales bus, ask a simple question: Is your salesperson a worker?

When I started in this business of sales consulting and training, I had a coach. The first area covered during our coaching sessions was my sales activity plan.

Initially, I thought this was a little strange because I mistakenly thought my coach would focus on my facilitation skills, helping me become a sage on the stage, a sales guru.

My coach recognized I could be the world's best speaker or trainer; however, like every other business, I needed to sell something before I could teach anything. I needed to do the work so I could do the work of helping people.

Look at your best salespeople. They do the work. Work ethic isn't old-fashioned—it's always in fashion. Great salespeople work hard at prospecting. They work hard at proactively asking for referrals and introductions. They work hard at account management and improving client relationships. They work hard at practicing new selling skills needed for success. Good salespeople do the work—and as a result, they reap the rewards of working with great clients.

A salesperson who isn't doing the work probably lacks a strong work ethic, passion, perseverance, or grit. Or, maybe the person simply doesn't like the profession of sales.

If you didn't hire a worker, it's time to fold 'em.

Growth or Grumbling

Growth and improvement in sales and life is achieved only through feedback. We've probably all pushed back at one time or another when hearing well-intended—and deserved—feedback. Egos get in the way. Self-doubt about our abilities shows up as false bravado and excuses. I certainly know I've been guilty of such behaviors.

A salesperson who is poised for growth will come back to their sales manager and say, "Hey, I appreciate your feedback and recognize my initial reaction was kind of defensive. Thanks for taking the time and here's what I am going to change up." That's a hold 'em salesperson, one who should stay on your sales bus.

Dr. Henry Cloud is the author of *Necessary Endings*. His book inspired the title for this chapter, as he offers great insights on the topic of letting go, which is often difficult.

I particularly liked the wisdom he offered around the difference between wise people—individuals who accept feedback and responsibility—and foolish people—those who demonstrate the exact opposite behaviors.

- Wise [salespeople] take in feedback and adjust accordingly.
  - Foolish [salespeople] get defensive when receiving feedback and immediately come back to you with a reason why "it" is not their fault. "I have a bad territory; the SDRs aren't qualifying the leads; we are having too many fulfillment issues."
- Wise [salespeople] own their performance, problems, and issues without excuses or blame.
  - Foolish [salespeople] immediately shift the blame to you and somehow make it your fault. "I haven't been given enough direction or training. We need better . . . everything!"

CEOs and sales managers: Are you trying to coach a wise salesperson or a foolish salesperson?

Dr. Cloud shares that if you have a foolish person on your team, stop talking. Stop giving feedback. These individuals can't or won't hear it.

Eliminate that growing bruise on your forehead.

Time to Fold 'Em

Many years ago, one of our Ei Selling® trainers, Michael, managed a successful sales team selling project management training. The company was growing and so was a sales management problem. One of his top salespeople was showing up to work late and not participating in group sales meetings. He was hitting his numbers but ignoring the values of the sales culture Michael was trying to create at the company.

Michael had several heart-to-heart conversations with his top producer, which produced little change. After several "foolish" coaching conversations, Michael let his top producer go. It wasn't an easy decision because of the sales being generated by this individual.

To his surprise, several members of his team thanked him for getting rid of their less-than-cooperative teammate. They respected Michael for his decision and were enthused by it. So much so that they quickly made up for the lost revenue being produced by the former foolish salesperson. It was a necessary ending that produced better beginnings of a strong sales culture.

Take time to think about your current sales team. Apply self-awareness and examine your own sales leadership behaviors. Is your hyper-responsibility making you more committed to success than your salesperson?

Apply the principles from the game of poker. Figure out which members of your team should stay on your sales bus. Which ones you should hold and which ones you should fold.

For more interview questions and hiring resources, go to www.EmotionalIntelligenceForSalesLeadership.com.

WHAT THEY DON'T TEACH YOU AT "TRADITIONAL" SALES MANAGEMENT SCHOOL

The role of most leaders is to get the people to think more of the leader but the role of the exceptional leader is to get the people to think more of themselves.

—Booker T. Washington

Everyone has an invisible sign hanging from their neck saying, make me feel important. Never forget this message when working with people.

—Mary Kay Ash

PART III

WHAT THEY DON'T TEACH YOU AT "TRADITIONAL" SALES MANAGEMENT SCHOOL

The Soft Skills, the Emotional Intelligence Skills of Effective Sales Leadership

IT WAS THE BEGINNING of our selling season and I put my road warrior hat on to begin weeks of travel with my sales team. There was one particular rep, who I will call Denise, that I was determined to help break through and achieve her sales goal. In prior years, she always came close but as the old saying goes, no sales cigar. She lived in a part of the country where it was difficult to find top sales talent so I really wanted to help Denise improve rather than look for a new salesperson.

I accompanied Denise on several appointments, observed sales calls, and offered sales coaching after each call. We debriefed what went well and what could have been improved. I followed up the day of travel with a note outlining selling activities and skills to continue or improve.

Fast-forward to the end of the year and I found myself looking at a territory that once again fell short of the goal. Why? Looking back, I realize that poor achievement of goal happened for two reasons:

I didn't have a people pipeline. I was guilty of falling into the instant gratification bucket of sales management. Instead of carving out time each week and month for recruitment and interviews, I settled for a below-average performer. Hope was my strategy rather than consistent prospecting for talent.

Like many sales managers, the coaching offered to Denise was focused on the mechanics of sales, selling techniques, and tips. "What other questions could you have asked? What do you think you did well? What would have been a better response to this question from the prospect?" I was focused on teaching and coaching Sales IQ, the hard skills of selling. Missing was education around the soft skills, the emotional intelligence skills of sales success. I was working on the wrong end of the sales performance issue. Today, I would change my coaching approach, recognizing that this salesperson wasn't good at time management and wasted two to three hours a day, costing her precious time that could have been directed to prospecting or client retention. The coaching conversation, held today, would provide tools and insights to improve her productivity habits.

Denise got easily triggered when conducting sales calls with challenging prospects. As a result, she'd talk too much and listen too little. Her lack of sales results wasn't just caused by poor selling skills. Today, I would work with Denise on the various tools and mindset needed for emotion management. That training would help her execute the right selling skills.

This is a far too common scenario in sales management. Hardworking, dedicated sales managers waste valuable coaching time because they are working on the wrong end of sales performance issues. They try to improve sales results by teaching more hard selling skills. In some cases, that is the fix. But in many cases, the root cause of poor sales performance is lack of emotional intelligence skills.

Now you might be thinking, wait a minute, I just read several chapters on hiring for soft skills, emotional intelligence skills. Why am I going to run into these selling challenges if I have conducted a thorough hiring process vetting for these skills?

You hired a human being. I have found in working with hundreds of sales teams and thousands of salespeople that demonstration of emotional intelligence skills can be situational. For example, a salesperson may possess a high degree of empathy. But once a quota is hanging over her head, empathy goes right out the window. She misses all the nonverbal communication going on in a meeting because her focus is on closing the deal rather than understanding the buyer's perspective.

A salesperson who presents solutions too soon is often provided more training around asking questions. Again, teaching these consultative selling skills might be the fix. But this salesperson may need more coaching around self-awareness. She knows the questions to ask, but lacks the patience to ask all the questions.

You've hired a young, new salesperson and taught him the importance of relationships and conversations. But he is a digital native and continues to email prospects and customers rather than picking up the phone. This salesperson doesn't lack selling skills. You have a salesperson who doesn't buy in or believe your approach is better. Coaching efforts need to focus on examining and changing his current belief systems around such connections and conversations. It won't do any good to hold one more conversation about the importance of building relationships.

Your role as a teacher and coach never stops, which means the learning for you never stops. Focus on learning the next set of skills to make you a more effective sales manager. Learn how to teach and coach soft skills, emotional intelligence skills.

Get to the Root Cause for
Poor Sales Performance

We received a call from a vice president of sales who had a salesperson that was "on the bubble." He was frustrated because the salesperson was at 60 percent of plan. This salesperson had been a top performer in her prior position, selling a similar product. The sales manager was providing coaching, with limited improvement. And in a very tight labor market, the vice president of sales was looking for any additional help to save this salesperson.

I assigned one of our Ei Selling® coaches, Rick, to this project. He's very good at teaching and coaching hard selling skills. But in this coaching engagement, he quickly discovered lack of soft skills was the root cause for lack of performance. The salesperson was struggling with self-limiting beliefs about herself. In her new role, she was calling on bigger titles and decision makers. She didn't think she had the ability to engage in meaningful conversations with high-level decision makers. Big office and big title syndrome were getting in the way of success. This salesperson was suffering from imposter syndrome, thinking that her prior success wasn't legitimate. On top of that, she was experiencing some family issues that were creating a lot of stress, affecting her ability to focus.

Fast-forward to the end of the coaching engagement and this salesperson was achieving 110 percent of quota. This salesperson did need some help in learning new and better selling skills. But what really changed her sales results was improving the soft skills holding her back—skills such as raising her self-awareness around limiting belief systems. She also benefited from education and insights on how to limit and control stress.

Coach to the right end of the sales performance challenge and you will coach to greater sales results.

Years ago, I read a great book authored by Mark McCormack, titled *What They Don't Teach You at Harvard Business School*. I could have easily titled this book, *What They Don't Teach You at "Traditional" Sales Management School*. While there are a lot of progressive universities now teaching emotional intelligence in their sales management programs, many managers did not attend these schools. Or, they attended school before such courses were offered and have not learned how to teach and coach the emotional intelligence skills needed for sales success.

The next section of this book isn't going to focus on teaching and coaching the mechanics of sales management such as sales pipeline management, pre-briefing calls, or debriefing calls. We offer such programs and there are a lot of great sales management books, blogs, and podcasts focused on this important area of sales leadership.

The next section of this book is to help sales leaders become better at teaching and coaching the soft skills, emotional intelligence skills, of sales success. Sales managers, welcome to what they don't teach you at "traditional" sales management school.

11

Emotion Management
and
Sales Effectiveness

WHAT DO A FORMER hostage FBI negotiator, NBA coach, and top sales producer have in common? The ability to manage their emotions in challenging situations. And in the sales profession, salespeople are going to run into more than their share of challenging prospects, customers, and sales conversations.

Chris Voss is a former FBI negotiator and author of *Never Split the Difference: Negotiating As If Your Life Depended On It*. When I initially picked up Chris's book, I was sure it would be full of examples of hard-nosed negotiating tactics. He discusses the hard skills of negotiation and bargaining skills that were important in his work with the FBI. But Voss also shares the importance of the psychological skills, the soft skills, needed in crisis intervention situations. He and his team members recognize the value of emotional intelligence, emotion management, and empathy in calming people down, establishing rapport, and gaining trust.

Phil Jackson, author of *Eleven Rings*, was a successful NBA coach. He led teams to eleven NBA titles, six with the Chicago Bulls and five with the Los Angeles Lakers. He's been referred to as the Zen coach because of his incorporation of meditation into the development of his players. According to Jackson, meditation is very beneficial for developing a great basketball team:

> Though mindfulness meditation has its roots in Buddhism, it's an easily accessible technique for quieting the restless mind and focusing attention on whatever is happening in the present moment. This is extremely useful for basketball players, who often have to make split-second decisions under enormous pressure. I discovered that when I had the players sit in silence, breathing together in sync, it helped align them on a nonverbal level far more effectively than words. One breath equals one mind.

You can hire the smartest salesperson in the room. However, if the individuals you hire are not able to manage emotions, it will impact their sales success. Just like a hostage negotiator or athlete, salespeople must have the ability to execute the right selling behaviors under pressure. They must have emotion management skills.

Avoid the Trigger-Response-Regret Loop

I have been a student of human behavior for a long time. But for many years, I was missing the knowledge about how emotions affected my ability to show up consistently and effectively.

I'd listen to the experts on positive affirmations, learning the power of positive self-talk. "I like myself. I am confident. I am calm." My library of self-help tools looked and sounded like something out of the old *Saturday Night Live* skits featuring Stuart Smalley.

Then, something or someone would show up and I would allow myself to get emotionally triggered. I'd respond in a manner that I would later regret. I call it the trigger-response-regret loop (see Figure 11.1).

FIGURE 11.1

As Ambrose Bierce said, "Speak when you are angry and you'll make the best speech you ever regret." And unfortunately, I've made a few of those speeches.

Emotion management is a skill that needs to be discussed, taught, and embraced by sales leaders. Without emotion management, good selling skills take a quick exit when a salesperson is in the middle of a crucial sales conversation. Increased education and focus on emotion management skills help salespeople avoid the trigger-response-regret loop.

How Does Emotion Management Affect Sales Results?

Let's look at a hypothetical selling situation. Your salesperson is meeting with three potential buyers. Two of the prospects love the salesperson. The third prospect—not so much. It's pretty easy to identify a prospect who doesn't love you. He gives short, grunt answers or sarcastic responses such as, "You're the expert . . . why don't you tell me." Or, the prospect deploys the new weapon of choice, bringing out the smartphone to return texts and messages as the salesperson is trying to run a high-level consultative sales meeting.

Without emotion management skills, it's very easy for a salesperson to get emotionally triggered and default to the emotional reactions of fight or flight.

A fight response is just what it sounds like.
- The salesperson gets defensive, and as a result, starts speaking louder and faster. This response breaks all the rules of rapport that you taught at your last sales meeting.
- The salesperson starts a product knowledge war with the prospect. She shares all her brilliant expertise because, by the time this meeting is over, this difficult prospect will realize just how little he actually knows. She wins the war on product knowledge and loses the sale.

A flight response is quite different.
- It looks like a scene out of the famous sales movie *Tommy Boy*. When a prospect pushes back with objections or pointed questions, it's easy for salespeople to default to "okey dokey" behavior. *I'm outta here. I don't get paid enough to put up with this behavior. I'll give you a call in a few . . . years!* Keep in mind, this behavior occurs after you have conducted a great workshop with your team on dealing with objections.
- How about this scenario: The texting prospect finally looks up and lobs a negotiation tactic at the salesperson. "You know, there are a lot of people looking to earn our business. Is this price the best that you can do?" The negotiation tactic emotionally triggers the salesperson and the regretful response is the discount dance. It sounds like a clip from the '70s Bee Gees song "Stayin' Alive." "Well, I think we can do 10 percent off the investment we discussed. Not working . . . 20 percent?" The salesperson is now negotiating with himself! Wait a minute, you just sent this salesperson to a negotiation sales training

workshop. And now he's discounting without any concession strategy?

Let's look at another sales scenario, one where positive emotions derail a sales meeting. Your salesperson meets with a pleasant, warm prospect who says all the right things. "This looks really interesting. We are always looking to improve. You know, if you're not getting better, you are getting beaten."

This is music to the salesperson's ears. Finally, an easy prospect, one who gets the value of what she is selling. In her enthusiasm, she tosses aside the company sales playbook. She skips over the qualifying questions and selling stages because she's "got one." The very nice prospect asks her to put something together to which the salesperson gives a resounding yes.

When she returns to present her solutions, the conversation suddenly changes. The positive, lovely prospect starts throwing out excuses such as, "We're actually doing pretty well. I need to run this up the ladder." Or the old standby excuse, "This is more expensive than I thought." (We want to get better but we don't want to invest any money to get better.) Another practice proposal buried in the proposal graveyard.

Many sales managers scratch their head and ask, "What happened to all that great training and knowledge I provided?" What happened is that emotions are running your sales team's meetings rather than effective selling and influence skills. It's the classic knowing and doing gap.

The Neuroscience of Effective Selling

Teach your sales team the hard skills, the consultative selling skills, Sales IQ. But devote equal time to teaching your sales team emotional intelligence skills, Sales EQ. One of the first concepts

I recommend teaching is the neuroscience of effective selling, emotion management.

You don't have to be a neuroscientist to teach these basic concepts to your sales team. Keep it simple and take your sales team on a high-level tour of the brain, starting with two areas that affect a salesperson's ability to consistently execute the right selling skills.

The first stop on the tour is the prefrontal cortex, often referred to as the executive center of the brain. This is where logical, rational thought resides. It's the part of your brain where intentional learning takes place and where problem-solving skills and good judgment reside.

The next stop on the tour is the amygdala, better known as the reptilian brain or lizard brain. This part of the brain was developed almost 200,000 years ago and it hasn't evolved much. Like the prefrontal cortex it has a job, and its number one job is to keep a person safe and alive. It's always scanning the environment, looking for threats. And here is where it gets interesting for salespeople and sales managers.

Under threat, perceived or real, the reptilian brain has the ability to override the logical brain, the prefrontal cortex. It's commonly referred to as the fight or flight response. When a sales call isn't progressing as planned, consultative sales training skills jump out the window, and negative emotions jump in the window, taking over the sales conversation.

Daniel Goleman is the social psychologist credited with bringing emotional intelligence out of academia and into the commercial world. He sums up this reaction well in his groundbreaking book, *Emotional Intelligence.* "When the amygdala is activated, it acts like a tripwire telegraphing a message of crisis to all parts of the brain. This messaging creates a series of physiological responses in the body."

One of those responses is the release of cortisol, a stress hormone, which affects clarity of thinking. Other responses are an increase in heart rate, breathing, and blood pressure. These nonproductive reactions set your salesperson up for a trigger-response-regret conversation.

We've all conducted a sales meeting and upon reflection asked ourselves the question, "Did I really say that? Oh, why didn't I say this?" It's because emotions ran the sales meeting rather effective selling and influence skills.

Salespeople with high emotion management skills are able to deliver peak performance on demand, regardless of the selling circumstance. Effective sales managers help their sales team understand the people, places, or situations that fire up their emotions and derail sales conversations.

Emotion Management and Self-Awareness

Emotion management is only improved with increased self-awareness. In the words of Socrates, "know thyself." Without self-awareness, salespeople (and sales managers) are bound to repeat the same mistakes because:

> **That which you are not aware of you cannot change.**

Teach and encourage your sales team to carve out quiet time in the morning, before their day starts. Give your sales team permission to check in with themselves before checking into any of their electronics.

It is only in the stillness that a salesperson gains clarity of thought. A chaotic mind is not a clear mind. A cluttered mind is not a clear mind. Improved self-awareness helps salespeople gain insights on people or situations that cause them to fall into the trigger-response-regret loop.

Share the following questions with your sales team to help them make better choices in their daily conversations with prospects, customers, and peers.

What triggers showed up yesterday that caused me to respond in a manner I regret?

- What can I do to change my response to that trigger?

Am I the trigger? Did my communication style, intensity, or tonality cause my prospects, customers, or peers to default to fight or flight responses?

- What can I change or adapt to create safe conversations rather than defensive conversations?

What difficult triggers will show up today in my interactions with peers, prospects, and clients?

- What will I do or say to make the outcome of the interactions move in a positive direction?

I've seen salespeople spend a lifetime running on the sales gerbil wheel, dealing with the same issues over and over. This behavior leads to exhaustion, burnout, and self-doubt. None of which helps a salesperson enjoy the profession of sales or earn more business.

During one-on-one coaching sessions or team meetings, continue to remind your sales team of the importance of carving out time for introspection and reflection. Repetition is the key to mastery, so keep repeating:

> That which you are not aware of you cannot change.
> That which you are not aware of you are bound to repeat.

Managing the Autobahn of Emotions

The reality is there will be times that a salesperson can't stop their immediate emotional reaction to a sales trigger because they haven't fully rewired their brains to respond differently.

It's similar to driving on the German autobahn. Speeding cars can suddenly appear out of nowhere and zoom past you at speeds exceeding one hundred miles per hour. The same thing happens with emotions because the reptilian brain responds in a nanosecond. It quickly speeds past a salesperson's logical brain and good judgment.

While a salesperson may not be able to immediately avoid a fight or flight response, you can teach your sales team how to limit their emotional response.

Reframing or reappraisal is a powerful tool that helps salespeople move from irrational, survival thinking to rational thinking and actions. Reappraisal allows people to change their interpretation of a situation. It's making a decision to put a new frame around an existing picture, perhaps an existing sales scenario.

When you dig deeper in the root cause of emotional reactions, you will find that most emotions are created by the stories salespeople tell themselves. We are all great writers of fiction and the main character in our stories is often fear. This emotion is great at generating the wrong actions or no actions. Fear generates negative emotions and negative sales results.

Salesperson's Story: "I'm New to This Industry"

Fear of being found out, being asked a question that the salesperson doesn't know the answer to. *Fear* that the prospect is going to know more than they do about the product or service. Salespeople avoid calling at the right level in the organization for *fear* of looking stupid. *Fear* is why they continue to meet with prospects who have no buying authority but appear safe.

Help salespeople reframe their stories. Change the story, change the emotional response, and you change the sales outcome. Create coaching questions that reframe a potentially fearful selling situation. The questions below elevate a salesperson's awareness around the negative stories—the false stories—they are telling themselves. *That which you are not aware of you cannot change.*

What's good about being new to the industry?
- I don't have biases and assumptions; therefore, I offer a fresh perspective.
- Since I am new, I am going to naturally be more curious and ask more questions and better questions. I don't even know enough to engage in a product dump!

What's the worst thing that can happen if you don't have the answer? What will be your response if you don't know the answer?
- I have a great team where I can find the answer and I can quickly follow up with the prospect or client. Since follow-up is one of the biggest complaints expressed by prospects and customers, I can control that activity.

Change the Question to Change the Emotion

It's difficult to manage emotions when a prospect or customer is being aggressive and, in some cases, in attack mode. The natural human response, spurred on by the survival brain, is to attack back or launch into defend and justify conversations.

Teach your sales team the power of the pause. Stop, step out of their shoes and into the shoes of their prospect or customer. Slow down and ask the powerful questions:

- What else is going on here?
- What's making this prospect or customer react or overreact?
- What is this person fearful about?

By asking these questions, the salesperson moves the conversation from their reptilian brain to their prefrontal cortex, the logical brain. Your salesperson will move from defensive behaviors to curiosity and even empathy.

- "I wonder if this prospect doesn't even know the right questions to ask. Maybe that's why he keeps asking about price."
- "Hmm . . . I wonder if this prospect is under a lot of pressure and I am the recipient of her stress?"

Change the question, you change the emotion and you change the resulting actions.

There is a wonderful scene in a movie where the concierge of a fine hotel is grooming his protégé on how to greet and manage their guests. He shares great advice for reframing conversations with upset guests.

"Remember, if one of our guests is upset, they really aren't upset. They are fearful. They are fearful they are not going to get the experience for which they paid."

This wise mentor was teaching his mentee empathy, which helped his mentee reframe conversations with upset customers. Empathy, rather than fear, allows his mentee to avoid the trigger-response-regret loop in challenging customer conversations.

It's important to teach your sales team that their biggest competitor in winning new business is not the obvious one, the known competitor. Their biggest competitors are sales ghosts of the past. Your prospects and customers have dealt with a number of salespeople over the years. Unfortunately, many salespeople overpromise and underdeliver. Often, when a prospect or customer is pushing hard, it's because they fear they will be taken advantage of. They resort to pushing because it's the only way they were able to get problems resolved in the past.

A great reframing question to teach your sales team is, "I wonder what sales ghost is showing up in this sales meeting?"

Ask powerful questions to change your sales team's emotional and nonproductive responses.

Take a Deep Breath

Upset customers, difficult questions from a prospect, certain negotiation tactics can trigger the reptilian brain. The body immediately responds, getting ready for fight or flight.

First responders, the military, and athletes employ tactical breathing to reduce stress and calm down. And in sales, there are a few sales meetings that feel like fire and combat!

Teach your sales team the power of breathing when they feel emotionally triggered. Something as simple as taking a few deep breaths sends a message to the arousal center of the brain, the reptilian brain, that everything is going to be okay. Breathing helps your salesperson get back in control so she can execute the right selling behaviors and skills, even in difficult selling situations. It even helps when holding a conversation with your spouse or kids!

Help your sales team remain emotionally *stable* so they are *able* to execute the right selling behaviors, even in difficult selling situations.

Sales Leaders EQ Action Plan

1. Teach your sales team the neuroscience of sales, emotion management. Train like a former FBI hostage negotiator and NBA coach.

2. Improve your sales team's emotional self-awareness. Encourage them to start their day with downtime and introspection. Stop repeating the same selling mistakes.
3. Enlighten your team around the power of reframing their stories.
4. Teach your sales team to manage their emotions by asking the powerful questions.
5. Don't forget to breathe!

12

Empathy
and
Influence

MANY YEARS AGO, I had a member of my team resign rather unexpectedly and unprofessionally. Now, this isn't one of those team members where you are silently saying, "Yay." This was a person that I had invested a lot of time, energy, and money in personal and professional development. I thought that the relationship between the two of us was solid, so the sudden departure was quite a surprise. I experienced many emotions with the sudden resignation.

The first was self-doubt. What kind of a leader am I that would cause a person to act this way? *Anger.* I can't believe anyone would do this. *Fear.* Who is going to do this person's work?

The next week I attended my monthly Vistage peer advisory group and shared my story. Great advice and support poured in. "Colleen, you're going to be fine. Every time I've had turnover, I've found an even better person for the position." "This might be a good time to redefine this position, rewrite the job description." "There is a lot of talent out there. You might be pleasantly surprised when you start searching for a replacement."

Then, a member of the group, HK, spoke up. He looked me right in the eyes, paused, and said, "Colleen, you just got kicked in the teeth. Doesn't feel very good, does it?"

At that moment, the conversation changed because I could actually *hear* the great advice. I could finally *feel* the support in the room.

The conversation changed because HK demonstrated empathy, stating what I was really thinking and feeling. He didn't use generic words like, "You must be frustrated," or "That must be really disappointing for you." No, he stepped into my mind, heart, and shoes and said exactly what I was feeling. I felt like I'd been kicked in the teeth.

This is one of the most important principles to teach your team when teaching empathy. People can't hear your advice until they feel like you've heard them. Prospects and customers are people and can't hear a salesperson's great solution until they feel like the salesperson has heard them.

The Challenge in Teaching Empathy

Each generation of sales leaders is presented with different challenges in achieving revenue. Empathy is first and foremost a paying attention skill and today's challenge is many salespeople and sales managers are losing their ability to pay attention. As a result, they lack the ability to demonstrate empathy.

One of today's biggest distractors affecting a person's ability to pay attention is the smartphone. For many people, it's become their adult binky. They don't go anywhere without it. The problem is that when a person has their adult binky in one hand, they are not paying *full* attention. They send a clear message to the other person that he or she is important—but not more important than any incoming message. Sadly, the new normal for many people is to conduct "half-conversations" with people. Half of the conversation is invested in speaking to the person, the other half of the conversation is spent glancing down at their cell phone for fear of missing . . . anything. Not a great stage for holding empathetic and deep conversations.

Let me say it again. (And again, and again.) Empathy is a paying attention skill and is developed only by carefully observing how your words and actions land on another human being. This requires looking up and around instead of down, staring at a computer, tablet, or cell phone. Empathetic salespeople are tuned into both verbal and nonverbal communication. Simply put, your salespeople must be present to win in order to create an emotional connection with prospects and customers.

In 2010, a team at the University of Michigan led by the psychologist Sara Konrath put together the findings of seventy-two studies conducted over a thirty-year period and found a 40 percent decline in the markers for empathy (measured as the ability to recognize and identify the feelings of others) among college students. Most of the decline took place after 2000, which led the researchers to link it to the new presence of digital communications. Sales leaders, it's time to change that statistic.

The Tuned-in Sales Team

How can a salesperson possibly influence another human being if she doesn't know, care, or demonstrate what her prospects and customers are thinking or feeling?

The short answer is, she can't.

We've all heard the buying principle, "People buy emotionally, not logically." It's important to take this phrase beyond the cliché it's become and really teach your sales team how the best salespeople and influencers make an emotional connection with prospects and customers.

Brene Brown, author of *Dare to Lead*, shares an important perspective in showing empathy.

> Understanding emotions in others and communicating our understanding of these emotions requires us to be in *touch with our own feelings.*

A salesperson with well-developed emotional literacy must first be in touch with his own emotions before he can recognize and respond to the emotional states of others. A salesperson can't tune into others until he has tuned into himself. It's the foundation of healthy relationships, both personal and professional.

That's why it's important for salespeople to carve out quiet time. It's only in the stillness that salespeople can tune into their emotions, what they are thinking or feeling. It's only in the stillness that salespeople can reflect on how their words and actions are landing on others.

Encourage your sales team to take a deeper dive into their emotions, because it's easy for all of us to default to easy, generic labeling of emotions. For example, I might say that I am angry—but with reflection and introspection, I recognize that I'm actually feeling disappointment. Salespeople say they are nervous but the reality is they are feeling intimidated, a very different emotion. A salesperson screws up a sales call and shares that she's upset. Dig a little deeper and you will find she's not upset; she's embarrassed by the face-plant she just experienced in front of a prospect. When a salesperson is tuned into her emotions, she moves beyond generic labeling of her own emotions. As a result, she's better at tuning into the real emotional temperature of prospects and clients. She's better at stating what a prospect or customer is really thinking or feeling.

Teach Real-World Empathy

Sales managers often miss the mark in teaching this powerful skill. They confuse empathy with validation or paraphrasing skills.

These listening skills are important throughout the sales conversation, but these skills are not empathy skills.

Validation or paraphrasing skills involve repeating what a prospect or customer says to ensure alignment. Empathy is saying what a person is thinking or feeling—and here's the challenge: *prospects and customers often don't say what they are thinking or feeling!*

Dr. Peter Drucker sums it up quite nicely: "The most important thing in communication is hearing what isn't said."

Here's an example of a salesperson applying validation skills instead of empathy skills. A salesperson meets with a prospect and the prospect shares her business problem, her pain. "We're really *frustrated* with slow response time from our current vendor. We aren't getting our phone calls or any email questions returned in a timely manner." The salesperson responds with validation skills and a hint of empathy. "I can understand why that is frustrating. So, if I'm hearing you correctly, you're tired of your current supplier not returning calls and emails quickly enough."

Ouch. This salesperson missed the opportunity to emotionally connect with the prospect. He simply repeated what the prospect said. He didn't say what the prospect was *really thinking or feeling.*

Empathetic salespeople are able to describe the underlying emotion a prospect is feeling and why they are feeling the emotion.

- Perhaps this prospect's frustration comes from feeling stupid because she allowed herself to be sold a bill of goods, and now she's stuck dealing with problems from choosing a lousy vendor.
- Maybe the prospect's frustration is pressure. "I'm spending all my time dealing with upset customers because this supplier keeps missing deadlines."
- The prospect's frustration is really self-doubt. "I thought I did a good job of vetting this company. Jeez, I don't

even know what questions to ask in order to make a better buying decision the next time."

A salesperson who is emotionally fluent tunes into the spoken *and* unspoken conversation. He tunes into his own emotions, recognizing times where he experienced similar thoughts and feelings. As a result, he's better able to demonstrate empathy when responding to a prospect's concern.

A better, more empathetic response might be, "Ms. Prospect, if I were sitting in your seat, I might be feeling like a victim of a classic sales bait and switch. You received a lot of promises from your current vendor, with few deliverables. And you also might be wondering if I'm going to tell you whatever you want to hear in order to earn your business. Am I reading this situation correctly?" The empathetic salesperson waits to hear a *yes* or *no*. Even if the answer is a *no*, my experience is that a prospect will open up, provide a correction to my statement, and share their true feelings.

Real-world empathy is saying what a prospect is *really* thinking or feeling. Empathy creates deeper sales conversations, ones that prospects and customers crave. They are tired of BS sales conversations, superficial conversations. They want to engage in real-world conversations.

Empathy creates an emotional connection with another human being. When a salesperson creates an emotional connection, she elevates the conversation. And when the conversation is elevated, the conversation changes—as does the business relationship.

Empathy changes the sales conversation.

Empathy, Objections, and Sales Elephants

When I started selling many years ago, I was taught to overcome the objection at least seven times. I really should go back and apologize to all the prospects I put through that painful process. Pretty sure their reptilian brains were shouting, "Danger, danger . . . this salesperson is never leaving this appointment without an order."

Fortunately, I learned a better way to deal with objections. And that better way is using my empathy skills to bring up potential objections. The empathetic salesperson tunes into what a prospect is *not saying* and proactively brings up potential concerns and objections. In our sales training workshops, we call it the sales elephant in the room. (We actually have a big stuffed elephant named Eddie we use during training workshops.)

Empathy is a key skill in dealing with objections. Stop teaching your sales team to overcome objections. Instead, teach your sales team to tune into the unspoken conversation, the unspoken objections. When a salesperson is put in a position of overcoming objections, he is playing defense, not offense. As a result, it's easy for a salesperson to push too hard, sending prospects into fight or flight responses. Their brains shut down—as does the conversation.

Salespeople who bring up the objection—particularly the unspoken objection, the sales elephant—elevate trust. The prospect thinks, "This salesperson really understands my world. He's just not trying to sell me. He gets my worries about making a change, investing dollars, working with a new vendor."

It eliminates superficial conversations, ones that dance around the real issues for changing, buying, or moving a deal forward.

Empathy, Influence, and Sales Results

Mary is a top performer for a recruiting firm. Her hard work pays off in securing a first meeting with a prospect who is not happy with their current provider of recruiting services. All the sales stars are lining up for an effective sales meeting. The prospect has a business problem and fits Mary's ideal client profile. She is meeting with the CEO, the power and economic buyer.

During the exploratory call, the prospect shares his pain around turnover and culture misfits. Mary does a great job of asking all of the consultative selling questions (Sales IQ), and the provocative questions during the meeting. The prospect is engaged, gives a lot of buying signals, but also mentions his worry about changing vendors. He asks Mary several questions about the size of her company, as their current recruiting firm is much larger than Mary's company. They decide to move forward and set up a second meeting, where Mary is confident that she can present a better plan for recruiting top talent.

During this meeting, the prospect doesn't seem quite as open as the first meeting. Mary is so intent on delivering her well-thought-out recommendations that she misses the emotional cues given from the prospect—the conversation that isn't happening.

The prospect is gracious and asks Mary for two days to think about the recommendations. Mary sets up a clear next step, connects with the prospect only to hear, "We've decided to stay with the existing recruiting firm."

What just happened? Mary brought great Sale IQ skills to the meeting, asking the right questions, meeting with the right buyer, uncovering budget. She set up clear next steps. What Mary didn't bring to the sales meeting was empathy—Sales EQ. She missed the sales elephants in the room, the unspoken objections.

Mary didn't step into the shoes of her prospect. The prospect recognizes that his current vendor might be average; however, his reptilian brain is fearful of change and the unknown. This part of the brain stepped into the decision-making process posing questions such as, "How do you know this new company is really going to be any better? They are a smaller staffing firm. Can they really meet the demands of a company our size?"

A better sales outcome may have resulted if Mary had tuned into what the prospect was really thinking or feeling when it came to switching vendors. "Jim, I'm getting the feeling you might have some concerns about changing vendors. And if I were sitting on your side of the table, I might have two worries. The perceived hassle of change . . . is it going to be worth it? And the size of our firm. Do we really have the resources to service your company? Am I reading this situation correctly?"

Now the conversation is about to change because Mary has stepped into the prospect's head, heart, and shoes. The conversation shifts from a superficial sales conversation to the real issues preventing a sale.

Remind your sales team they don't have to agree with another person's perspective to demonstrate empathy. What they do have to do is work hard at seeing the world from that person's perspective. How can you influence another human being if you can't state what they are thinking or feeling?

You can't.

Don't Miss the Meeting after the Sales Meeting

Be aware that when you teach the concept of proactively bringing up the sales elephant, your sales team will get nervous. They will object to this approach! Salespeople mistakenly think that bringing up objections will derail the sales call. Nothing could be further from the truth. Salespeople who don't pay attention to the dynamics occurring during a sales conversation miss the meeting after the sales meeting.

You know the one I'm talking about.

The salesperson wraps up the meeting and leaves. The next meeting occurs, the real meeting. The decision makers get together and start addressing their fears and concerns about switching vendors, investing more money, or making a purchase. This meeting occurs *without* the salesperson present to facilitate the sales conversation. And often, these conversations are based on false information, perceptions, or a prior bad experience with another salesperson.

Fears include:

- Is the timing right?
- Can we afford the business disruption?
- How do we know if this vendor can really deliver?
- They are a small company . . . can they really deliver services to an organization our size?
- They are a big company . . . are we going to be just another number to them?
- They haven't done a lot of work in our industry . . . are we going to spend time and money getting them up to speed on our business?
- I wonder if we can do this ourselves.
- They've only been in business five years. Are they financially stable?
- Their services are more expensive. Will we get the ROI?
- And the list goes on . . .

I have closed more than one business deal because I applied empathy and tuned into the emotional cues being given by the prospect, which resulted in discussion around the sales elephant in the room.

In fact, I remember my first sales call where I finally had the self-awareness, empathy, and let's throw in courage to bring up the sales elephant.

The Sales Elephant
in the Board Room

Years ago, I was referred into a law firm by one of my referral partners with the goal of improving the firm's business development strategies and skills. The meeting was held in a beautiful boardroom with eight partners of the firm. We had a good dialogue around training objectives and outcomes. Then, the conversation moved from a dialogue to a cross-examination. One of the partners wanted to know if I could guarantee results. He asked several questions about my "sales degree." He wanted references speaking to my credibility and results. I knew this buyer was a high analytical and needed a lot of data. But I also knew that there was an unspoken objection in the room that needed to be dealt with. "I am happy to provide references; however, let's talk about the real challenge your firm needs to tackle before you sign up for any kind of business development training. Everyone in your firm bills out at $350 to $600 an hour. The real problem isn't going to be our training methodology or my expertise. What I teach works—if the client does the work. The real problem will be convincing members of your team to attend training. I'm guessing there will be a few individuals who will view the training as costing them money rather than making them money." The sales elephant was sitting in the middle of that beautiful table, trunk raised. *Silence.* Then laughter broke out because the partners knew I was right. We ended up working together and I am sure one of the main reasons for winning the business was because I was willing to bring up the unspoken objection. I didn't miss the meeting after the meeting.

Teach, Practice, Repeat

Repetition is the key to mastery, and improving empathy takes a lot of repetition. I love the blocking and tackling side of pre-briefing and debriefing sales calls, the mechanics of sales coaching.

"What has the prospect tried to do to fix this problem?"

"Where else is this business problem affecting the prospect?"

"How committed is the prospect to making a change?"

"What is their decision process when purchasing . . . ?"

Equally important to include in your coaching sessions is empathy coaching. Keep reminding your sales team to step out of their sales shoes and into the shoes of their prospects and clients. Design coaching questions that raise self-awareness, other awareness, and improve empathy skills.

"What do you think is the prospect's biggest worry in changing vendors?"

"Our services are new and innovative. What do you think your prospect's biggest concern is when buying a service that hasn't been field-tested for ten years?"

"It sounds like your decision maker is really swamped at work. What's a day in the life like for this person? Even if they logically know they should make a change, how is their reptilian brain going to react to the perception of more work?"

"How is your personality style affecting the conversation? Are you adapting or sending prospects into fight or flight responses?"

Empathy is a powerful influence skill, one that takes time, training, and repetition to master. Make empathy training a part of your sales training process. How can you influence another human being if you don't know or care about what they are thinking or feeling?

You can't.

Sales Leaders EQ Action Plan

1. Improve your sales team's emotional self-awareness. Ask them to identify their emotions to better tune into the emotions of prospects and customers.
2. Model and teach the value of paying attention.
3. Teach your sales team the difference between paraphrasing and real-world empathy.
4. Teach your sales team the power of empathy first, advice and solutions second.
5. Include empathy coaching questions in your sales call debriefs.

13

What Do Your Salespeople Believe?

ONE OF THE MOST classic stories of belief systems driving actions and results is the story of Roger Bannister. He made headlines around the world by being the first person to run a mile in less than four minutes, 3:59:4 to be exact. Up until that point, people "believed" that it was physically impossible for a human being to run that fast.

But here's where it gets interesting. Bannister's record lasted only forty-six days because Australian John Landy beat it by running a 3:57:9 mile. And since that time, over 1,400 athletes have broken the four-minute mile.

What changed? Did great runners suddenly change their training regime? Were superior athletes suddenly coming of age? The number one thing that changed performance outcomes was the belief that running a four-minute mile could be accomplished. The number one thing that shifted was the former negative self-talk surrounding this goal. "No way this can be done" changed to "Well, if he can do it, maybe I can as well."

Sales managers, your sales team may not be trying to run a four-minute mile. But they are trying to run a better race in sales—and many are not winning the race because of their limiting belief systems.

Some of you reading this chapter might be thinking that this belief system, positive self-talk stuff, is little bit "woo woo."

Perhaps it's time to challenge *your* belief systems.

According to research from the Harvard Business School, just uttering the three words "I am excited" in a high-pressure situation is proven to relieve stress, improve self-confidence, and lead to better performance.

Research among athletes and students shows that improving positive self-talk results in improved performance by a number of measures. Stephen Cheung, an environmental physiologist and avid Cyclo-cross competitor, conducted a study in 2016. He gave cyclists two weeks of positive self-talk training before an intense ride in a heat chamber at 95 degrees Fahrenheit. He taught the cyclists to replace negative thoughts such as "I'm boiling" with motivational statements like, "Keep pushing, you're doing well." This positive self-talk lengthened their time to exhaustion from eight minutes to over eleven minutes.

Sales managers devote a lot of time to reviewing sales pipelines, conducting win/loss discussions, and engaging in role-plays to improve sales results. But often, sales managers don't help salespeople develop the skills needed to win against their *biggest competitor*: identifying and changing self-limiting beliefs.

When you hire a salesperson, you also hire their belief systems. They show up to your office with two briefcases. One briefcase is visible, full of business and sales acumen (see Figure 13.1).

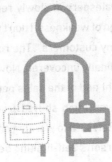

FIGURE 13.1

The other briefcase is invisible. It's stuffed full of beliefs a salesperson has learned—or otherwise absorbed—from parents, teachers, coaches, siblings, colleagues, and friends. Some of these beliefs serve salespeople well. Other beliefs need to be challenged and changed in order to help your salesperson achieve peak performance.

Beliefs Drive Actions

One of our clients discovered the importance of uncovering his sales team's self-limiting beliefs. He had a salesperson on his team who was bright and funny. Clients loved him and his work. However, this salesperson wasn't great at prospecting so the sales manager was having yet another coaching session with him on tactics and strategies to fill the sales pipeline.

My client was puzzled because he had provided this salesperson with really good training around asking for referrals. This was a natural prospecting strategy for this salesperson because of his raving fan client base. And yet, the salesperson wouldn't ask for referrals. When asked, his usual response was, "Uh, I forgot." After attending our sales management workshop, the sales manager tried another approach. He stopped teaching, telling, and reviewing information on asking and receiving referrals. He moved his focus to understanding this salesperson's belief system. "What's making you uncomfortable about asking for referrals?" The salesperson slowly replied, "In my family, asking for help is a sign of weakness. I don't want to appear weak or needy in front of my customers." The root cause for lack of sales execution was finally uncovered. Now the sales manager could work on the right end of the sales performance issue.

The coaching conversation shifted from teaching tactical sales training skills (Sales IQ) to working on the right end of the problem, the salesperson's self-limiting beliefs around asking for help (Sales EQ).

You are the Chief Belief Officer. One of your many roles as a sales leader is helping your sales team believe in themselves, the company, and the products or services they are selling. Selling skills are important—but equally important is raising your sales team's self-awareness around limiting self-beliefs that affect sales results.

That Which You Are Not Aware of You Cannot Change

Remember the movie *Hoosiers*, in which Gene Hackman portrayed real-life coach Marvin Wood? Coach Wood guided the Milan High School Indians to the Indiana state basketball championship and a 28–2 record in 1954. This movie is a great example of self-limiting beliefs and how one man changed an entire basketball team's belief in themselves and their abilities.

Milan, with an enrollment of only 161 students, really had no business going so far in the state tournament. (So many people believed.) In the final game, the Indians faced powerhouse Muncie Central, a much larger school.

Wood knew his small-town team might get intimidated playing against a bigger school in a much larger arena at Hinkle Field House. They might believe they didn't stand a chance of winning based solely on the size of their school, rather than the size of their talent.

I believe Wood used his emotional intelligence to understand his team's mindset. He stepped into his players' shoes, applied empathy, and really tried to understand what his team was thinking or feeling. He focused on managing his team's mindset and beliefs, rather than running one more basketball drill.

When his team arrived at Hinkle Field House, which was triple the size of Milan's hometown gym, he gave his players a measuring tape and told them to measure the basketball floor. They discovered there was no size difference from their home court. They had played on this size court before *and* they had won on this size court. He changed any self-limiting beliefs about the size of the court—and the size of the opponent—which changed their ability to effectively execute their basketball skills and beat the four-time state champion Muncie Central Bearcats. Beliefs drive actions, skills, and outcomes.

It might be time to get out your tape measure and check out what belief systems are holding your sales team back from playing the game of sales to the best of their ability.

The size of the court for your team might be:

- *The size of the opportunity.* "This deal is too big for me to pursue and close."
- *The size of the competition.* "They are five times our size. We don't stand a chance."
- *The size of the learning.* "I've never been in this selling scenario before. I don't know what the heck I'm doing."

Devote time in your one-on-one coaching sessions to learn, examine, and increase your sales team's self-awareness around beliefs that are holding them back in the game of sales.

Self-Limiting Beliefs about Themselves

Self-limiting beliefs are formed from repeated thoughts and self-talk. Say something to yourself long enough and it becomes a belief, a person's truth. Open up that invisible, self-limiting briefcase and you will find a compartment filled with negative self-talk about a salesperson's own abilities or attributes. Here are a few that I've heard over the years:

- People don't take me seriously because I am a woman.
- Men aren't good listeners because we lack empathy.

- I'm too young to call on the C-suite.
- I'm too old to learn these new digital selling tools.
- I'm an engineer . . . I'm not good at sales.
- I don't have an advanced degree so I can't call on doctors.
- I'm disorganized.
- I don't have enough time to . . .
- I'm an introvert and not good at small talk . . .
- And the list goes on.

Beliefs drive the actions a salesperson will take or not take. They drive the skills a salesperson will learn and apply. Sales managers work with their sales teams designing sales activity plans. Time is invested in skill development. The problem is that a self-limiting belief impacts the execution of both the plan and the skills.

I can't tell you how many times I've heard self-limiting beliefs around age. A young sales professional complains, "I'm young. No one is going to take me seriously." The "I'm too young" salesperson gets easily intimidated by calling on buyers who are her senior. She doesn't believe this prospect will take her seriously. And sure enough, her negative self-talk turns into a self-fulfilling prophecy. She shows up to meetings lacking confidence, which in turn makes the prospect wonder if the product or service is really worth the investment. Lack of confidence is the reason the salesperson didn't win the business, not her age.

On the opposite side of the age equation are veteran salespeople. Their limiting self-beliefs range from, "I've been at this selling game a long time . . . I've got this." Or, "I'm too old to learn and master new tools for success." Veteran salespeople don't attend sales training courses because, well, they've got this. Some give a half-hearted attempt to master new selling or technology tools because their core belief is that you can't teach an old sales dog a new sales trick. Beliefs drive actions and the result is no change and stagnant sales.

Believe It or Not

I've always felt very fortunate to have good bosses and mentors in my life, many that raised my self-awareness around self-limiting beliefs.

One of my first jobs out of college was working at the American Cancer Society in Minneapolis, Minnesota. I started as an assistant to the executive in charge of fundraising for the state. Carol was a terrific boss. One day, as were wrapping up a meeting, she said, "You are one of the most organized assistants I have ever had." I responded with disbelief. "No, I'm actually disorganized." She smiled and responded, "No, that would be incorrect. I've had a lot of assistants and you are right at the top."

Game changer. My belief system up to that point was that "I would lose my head if it wasn't attached." This message came from my family and rightly so. I was that kid who was constantly leaving coats, sweaters, or scarves someplace. Not too much has changed in that category. If I'm not careful, I can still manage to lose one coat a year during my travels. (I've since learned that losing apparel is not the same as being disorganized.)

My boss changed my self-talk. I started looking at myself through a different lens, seeing how organized I was. And because I believed I was organized, I became even more organized. This piqued my interest on the topic of productivity, which developed into strong time-management habits that I continue to use today to be successful and less stressed in business.

Sales Management Self-Awareness Question: Do you know and understand self-limiting beliefs that might be holding your salespeople back from sales success?

Self-Limiting Beliefs about the Company

I've observed self-limiting beliefs around a salesperson's attitude toward the company. The negative self-talk ranges from, "We're too big," to "We're too small," to "We're too new." These limiting beliefs result in salespeople blaming the company for their lack of success, rather than looking at their own selling skills and daily selling behaviors. The constant negative self-talk becomes their truth.

- "Our smaller competitors are more agile than my big, slow-moving company." Beliefs drive actions. This salesperson doesn't believe she can do anything to impact the outcome of a sales conversation. She gives up before she even shows up to the sales appointment.
- "We're small . . . we don't have the resources to handle bigger prospects or clients." Beliefs drive actions. So, this salesperson doesn't even pursue bigger deals. He doesn't even give himself the opportunity to lose!
- "We're new . . . no one wants to do business with an unknown entity in the market." The first time salespeople hear a prospect say, "We haven't heard of your company before," they get extremely nervous. Instead of showing conviction and strength around their product and services, they immediately discount the price to win the business.

David and Goliath

When I started in sales with Varsity Spirit Corporation, our biggest competitor was about eight times our size. It was the classic David and Goliath story. The good news is that many of the early members of the sales team were new to sales. We didn't even know enough to be nervous about the size of the competition! Ignorance is bliss. We didn't worry about being the underdog because of our conviction in the company, our products, and our services.

I remember receiving my first sales report, summarizing the accounts in my territory of Iowa and Nebraska. There were around six hundred accounts, of which Varsity was conducting business with very few. In reviewing the report, I didn't panic because—ignorance is bliss. My self-talk was positive. "Well, with six hundred accounts, surely I can open up at least forty new accounts this year." And guess how many new accounts I opened up my first year in sales? Forty new accounts. Beliefs drive actions, skills, and outcome.

Looking back, I'm grateful that I wasn't exposed to any negative salespeople who could have filled my head with self-limiting beliefs.

"You are the new kid on the block. It's going to take you a long time to unseat the competitor."

"The competition has better brand awareness. Prospects are going to be reluctant to work with you. You'll probably need to discount to get a foot in the door."

Even in my early years of sales, I had good self-awareness. I knew I wasn't that good at sales. However, I believed I could outwork and out-service my competition. Those beliefs—not my average selling skills—opened up new accounts.

Sales Management Self-Awareness Question: Do you know and understand the limiting beliefs your sales team may have about the company and how those beliefs are affecting their sales success?

Self-Limiting Beliefs about Your Company's Products and Services

We live in the information age, the technology age where it's easier than ever to copy and duplicate products and service offerings. In an increasingly commoditized world, salespeople often start believing that they don't have a differentiator. As a result, they default to poor selling behaviors such as discounting. They give unnecessary concessions in order to win business. We do a lot of work in these industries so I am familiar with the "we're a commodity" story.

Well-intended sales managers try to solve these selling behaviors by teaching more consultative selling skills and negotiation skills. In some cases, this education will fix the selling on price problem.

However, in many situations, the sales manager needs to look further. The root cause of discounting might stem from your sales team's belief systems and convictions around your products and services.

Conviction and Sales Results

I was working with a sales team in the furniture space. The VP of sales asked me to interview his top salesperson, Diaz, to see if I could figure out exactly what he was saying or doing as he was selling the top-of-the-line furniture at a profitable margin. After the interview, he wanted me to document what Diaz was saying or doing so we could incorporate it into the company's sales playbook.

I sat down, eager to learn this salesperson's secret selling sauce. I was expecting him to share provocative questions, challenging questions, insight selling, pre-call planning insights, closing skills. Instead, what I heard was a salesperson with deep conviction about the value he provided. His success was driven from positive beliefs around his products and services.

"I think I sell a lot because I really believe our target clients need a quality product. They don't want to purchase furniture every other year. Our clients put in long days so they need good, ergonomic furniture. If they don't have the right type of furniture and environment, it affects their ability to be productive. And that costs the company money. So, I actually don't even discuss our less expensive lines of furniture. It's not what they need."

The notes added to the company sales playbook were very short.

"Believe in your products and services."

Sales Management Self-Awareness Question: Do you know and understand the limiting beliefs your sales team may have about your products and services and how it's affecting their sales success?

How to Improve Self-Limiting Beliefs and Negative Self-Talk

Okay, you've diagnosed a salesperson's self-limiting belief. Now the hard work begins. It's difficult to change belief systems for a variety of reasons. Once a person develops a core belief, they pay close attention to anything that reinforces that belief. It's called belief perseverance. When a person believes something, they filter out evidence to the contrary. Look at the newspapers people subscribe to. Do people read papers that support their current beliefs or challenge their current beliefs? How about news channels? Do you listen to a news channel that supports your current beliefs or challenges you to think in new ways?

I remember working with an underperforming salesperson who believed he didn't have time to prospect. But he always seemed to find time to study his cheaper competitors' price points. That data supported his belief system that his company's products were too high-priced. (Never mind that other salespeople on his team were closing business at full margin.)

Coaching self-limiting belief systems requires delayed gratification skills as shifting beliefs may not be a quick fix. It requires pre-call planning questions that are different than those used for pre-briefing or debriefing sales calls.

Perception or Actual

It's important to figure out if your salesperson's limiting belief is based on perception or past experience. The correct diagnosis helps you coach and provide the right solution to the problem.

Perception is a way of regarding or interpreting an event or situation. The problem is the interpretation isn't based on data or facts. Beliefs based on perception evolve from the stories a salesperson has told himself over and over about a selling scenario. Tell yourself a story long enough and the story moves from fiction to nonfiction. Perception becomes a salesperson's reality, their truth.

It's tempting to tell a salesperson that their perception is false. Go back to the basic principles of effective sales. If you are telling, you are not selling—and the same principle applies in coaching. People believe their own data so if you are telling during a coaching session you are not "selling" the salesperson on a new way of looking at a situation.

One of the coaching tools I use to shift perception and false stories is pivot questions. These coaching questions make a salesperson stop, pivot, and say, "Huh, I never thought of that perspective. Hmm . . . might be a new way of looking at this selling scenario." Pivot questions help a salesperson discover a new truth, a new story, and a more positive belief.

Here are a few pivot questions that challenge perceptions.

Scenario One

Salesperson: *"No one knows who we are so I can't even get a conversation opened up."*

Pivot Questions

- *"Is that based on perception or data?"* (Be ready to explain the difference.)
- *"Is it the brand that opens up most sales conversations or the relevance of the prospecting messages to the potential buyer?"* (Raise self-awareness around the quality—or lack of quality—of the seller's prospecting outreaches.)
- *"How many well-known brands started out in business being the unknown brand? What do you think those salespeople did to create opportunities?"* (A great question that helps the salesperson realize that every company has been an unknown brand at some point in the life cycle of their company.)

Scenario Two

Salesperson: *"Our prices are just too high."*

Pivot Questions

- *"Are our prices too high or are you calling on the wrong prospects?"* (Great question to help the salesperson discover she needs to invest more time in identifying and targeting the right prospects.)
- *"We do have clients that are paying full margin. What is the common pain point that we solve for them and how do we find more of those buyers?"* (This question eliminates victim mentality and lack of control.)

- *"Is the prospect actually saying that or are you thinking that?"* (You'd be surprised at how many times you will hear a salesperson say, "Uh, no . . . but . . .")

Perception is reality and as the Chief Belief Officer of your company, it's your job to coach your sales team to recognize false realities and create new ones. They are making up stories about a selling situation so why not help them create better stories!

When the Past Drives the Future

A past failure or bad sales call can easily become a salesperson's new truth. "I don't know enough. I'm not good enough. I need more training . . ."

Never underestimate how often failure inhibits salespeople from executing the right selling behaviors. For example, you've taught, coached, and told your sales team the value of calling on the C-suite. You've preached, "This is where decisions are made and money is invested."

However, the last time your salesperson Joe called on a big title and big office, he got stumped by the questions asked from the *big* prospect. He felt embarrassed and intimidated, and has rehearsed that failed sales call over and over, like a bad rerun. Based on this onetime event, Joe's new belief is that he's not good enough to hold conversations with C-suite buyers.

The salesperson's reptilian brain adds to his fear of failure. The reptilian brain is all about avoiding danger. And in this case, the reptilian brain tells the salesperson to play it safe, avoid those big buyers in the C-suite. It's not logical thinking, but remember, the reptilian brain isn't operating on logic. It's operating on emotion, and feeling stupid is not a great emotion to go forth and conquer the next sales call.

Self-Awareness and Coaching

Apply the EQ skill of self-awareness and examine your go-to response as a sales manager. If you're like me, my first response is to teach Joe more tactical, consultative selling skills on how to effectively engage with the C-suite buyer.

Stop and think. Address the real issue, which is Joe's self-limiting belief around not being good enough or smart enough. Apply empathy and step into Joe's shoes and think about his self-talk after this recent face-plant. His negative chatter might include, "They know more than I do. I'm not ready to handle this size of deal. Big titles are tough people to deal with. These people don't respect salespeople." Joe is not going to do well on his next sales call carrying that briefcase full of self-limiting beliefs.

People believe their own data. Take time to design coaching questions that help your "Joe" discover different answers and positive self-talk.

First, apply empathy and state what your salesperson is thinking or feeling. "Boy, that must have been a difficult meeting . . . I've had a few of those myself. I'm guessing you might even be wondering if you even want to call on larger accounts." Once you hear a yes from the salesperson, ask permission to further explore. Empathy first, advice second. Create questions that help your salesperson discover that he will live to sell another day.

- What lessons did you learn from this difficult sales meeting?
- How will you apply the lessons learned to set yourself up for success on the next call?
- Are you smarter because of this bad call?
- What's the worst thing that can happen if you don't know the answer to a question on future calls?
- What can you do to be better prepared for the next call?

- What do you think *big* decision makers want? (Answer: Confidence. Honesty. No BS.)
- How do you think your reptilian brain is playing into your success? What can you do to improve your mental pre-call planning for the next sales meeting?

Great sales managers and coaches are like great doctors. They're good at diagnosing the root cause for poor selling performance, which helps them prescribe the right coaching solutions.

Belief Systems and the Power of Storytelling

Augment your coaching efforts with stories of people who have overcome the odds by believing in themselves and not believing in the naysayers. Stories are a great teaching tool because the brain is wired to remember stories.

A great story about the power of positive self-talk and belief in one's ability is that of Diana Nyad. Nyad has a long list of accomplishments. In 1975, she set a speed world record by swimming around Manhattan in less than eight hours. Her 102.5-mile swim from the Bahamas to Florida broke records set by both men and women. But her dream was swimming the 110 miles between Havana and Key West. She tried several times and failed because of jellyfish attacks, asthma attacks, and weather. Finally, on her fifth try, she achieved her dream, becoming the first person to swim from Cuba to Florida without a shark cage or fins. She was sixty-four years old.

Can you imagine how many people told Diana she was too old to try this swim at age sixty-four?

"Diana, come on, give it up. You're on the back nine of your swimming career."

She had failed at four prior attempts.

"Diana, you gave it your best shot. It's just not in the cards for you. Take up the game of golf."

Diana Nyad was successful not only because of her athleticism but also because of her strong belief in herself and her abilities. Watch her TED talk or listen to interviews and you will hear her positive self-talk. Her mantra, and the title of her book, is *Find a Way*.

Find a Way is a great belief system to instill in your sales team. Teach your team the power of positive affirmations and acting as if they've already achieved their goals. Whatever you say to yourself long enough becomes a belief, becomes your truth.

Use Diana's Find a Way positive self-talk to help your team get started.

1. I will find a way to consistently execute my sales activity plan.
2. I will find a way to improve my selling skills every day.
3. I will find a way to emotionally connect with everyone I speak to each day.
4. I will find a way to achieve my sales goal with ease and grace.
5. I will find a way to be happy and optimistic every day.
6. I will find a way to manage my emotions.
7. I will find a way to attract great people into my life.

Imagine the sales results your team would achieve by writing and saying these affirmations every day. It's time to add one more sales metric to the sales activity plan. Set a metric for your team to listen to or read positive and motivational information every day. Beliefs drive sales results. What does your sales team believe?

Sales Leaders EQ Action Plan

1. Evaluate each person on your sales team. What positive beliefs are driving their actions or selling behaviors?

What negative beliefs are impacting their sales performance?

2. Develop coaching questions to help each salesperson discover limiting beliefs that are holding them back.
3. Pick up Keith Rosen's book *Sales Leadership*. He's developed a lot of great coaching questions for sales managers.
4. Teach your team the power of positive self-talk. Find stories to support your training.
5. Apply self-awareness. What skills do you need to learn or improve in order to better coach your team on self-limiting belief systems? Telling is not selling or influencing.
6. Examine your own belief systems. How convicted are you about yourself, your company, and the products and services you offer?

14

You Don't Make Mistakes. Mistakes Make You

THE MOVIE *THE LAST WORD* depicts the story of a retired successful businesswoman, Harriet Lauler. Due to a medical condition, Harriet has little time left before her imminent death. In her typical, take-charge fashion, she engages a young, local newspaper reporter, Anne Sherman, to write her obituary before she dies to ensure her life story is told her way. Yes, you read that sentence correctly. She engages the reporter before she dies. That is what I call pre-call planning!

In one of their many lively dialogues, Lauler gives a piece of advice to the aspiring journalist: "You don't make mistakes. Mistakes make you." Great advice for everyone, particularly sales professionals.

Most salespeople have heard the phrase, "You learn more from your failures than your successes." It sounds good, but look around. Most people avoid failure like the plague. And often, sales managers and sales organizations send conflicting messages to their sales team around failure.

Walk into the reception area of an office and you will see a wall filled with plaques, trophies, and pictures touting the company's successes. Vendor of the year, salesperson of the year, fastest growing company in the world. Now, look further in the office suite to see if you can find a failure wall—you know, the one that shows all the company's failures and the invaluable lessons learned from failure.

> If failure is our greatest teacher, why isn't there some kind of wall devoted to listing the failures and the many valuable lessons learned that helped the company grow and improve?

I'm being a little facetious. However, sales managers need to examine how their actions—or lack thereof—deliver another message to their salespeople.

Implications from Fear of Failure

There are many implications to achieving consistent sales results when sales managers "fail" to teach their salespeople how to "fail well." Here are a few I've observed and I am sure you will be able to add to this list.

1. Salespeople who fear failure take noes from prospects personally. They feel rejected, which creates the emotion of self-doubt and "I'm not good enough" self-talk. This in turn leads to limited risk-taking. Instead of calling on new and better accounts, the ones you discussed in your last coaching session, salespeople continue to work with safe, existing clients or pursue easy, comfortable deals.
2. Salespeople worried about failing don't apply new selling skills received from their sales manager or sales training. They fall into the perfection trap and keep getting ready to get ready. Their goal (and fear) is to avoid looking and sounding stupid. The reality is, a salesperson can

practice—a lot—but the sales rubber really hits the road only when the salesperson is demonstrating the new selling skill in front of live prospects and customers.

3. Salespeople worried about failing turn into professional people pleasers. They go-along-to-get-along, trying to say and do what will gain acceptance from prospects, many times at the expense of a sale. A professional people pleaser avoids asking difficult questions during a sales meeting for fear of not being liked. They believe if they please people all the time, it will help them avoid the pain of rejection (failure). Professional people pleasers over-promise and then get stuck with the mess of trying to explain why the company couldn't deliver.

4. Fear of failure salespeople push back on feedback. They fall into the performance, perfection trap. Their self-worth is based solely on their performance in life, not on their character or values. You've probably been a part of this drill if you've been in a sales leadership role long enough. You accompany a salesperson on several calls, in person or on the phone. A few selling mistakes are made and you give well-intended feedback. The fear of failure salesperson takes the feedback personally and reacts with, "Yeah but . . ." excuses instead of thanking you for the help.

5. Failure-averse salespeople don't set goals. If they set a goal, they may not achieve the goal, which in their eyes equates to failure. These salespeople subscribe to the crazy thinking of, "I don't win big so I never lose big." Research shows that people who write down goals, review goals, and share goals have a much better chance of achieving goals. I have seen really talented salespeople not hit their full potential because they avoid setting goals in order to avoid feeling like a failure. There is a great scene from the movie *Chariots of Fire*. Harold Abrams, the English runner, competes

against Eric Liddell, the Scottish champion, and loses for the first time in his life. He takes the loss personally and the pain of failure is so great he decides not to run again. His girlfriend, Cybil, challenges Harold on his decision not to run, to which he replies, "I don't run to take a beating—I run to win!" Cybil's response is perfect. "If you don't run, you can't win."

Failure-averse salespeople adopt a similar philosophy. They don't even show up to the race. As a result, you dread giving feedback and start avoiding the crucial sales coaching conversations. You logically understand it's your role and responsibility to help this salesperson grow. All the sales management books tell you that feedback is the breakfast of champions. (No thanks, you would rather wait for lunch.) Without feedback, the salesperson settles into "good enough" selling behaviors, which creates good enough sales cultures. The problem is, good enough isn't good enough to win and retain business in today's competitive environment.

Moving Failure beyond Lip Service

What can sales managers do to improve their team's resiliency and ability to power through mistakes and setbacks? How do the best sales leaders create risk-taking, failure-loving, lessons-learned sales teams?

Develop the emotional intelligence skill of self-regard with each member of your team. Self-regard is the ability to admit strengths and weakness. And when salespeople can admit and accept their mistakes, then and only then do they learn the valuable lessons gained from risking and making mistakes. Salespeople with high self-regard have more success because they have the ability and confidence to learn from their failures, rather than get defeated by their failures.

The number one concept I teach salespeople and sales managers is the importance of separating their role performance from their self-worth, the person they are.

My first exposure to this concept was working as an associate for Sandler Sales Institute. The founder, David Sandler, preached the importance of separating your *identity* in life from your *role* in sales. Since then, I have heard ministers and personal development gurus deliver a similar message. Separate what you *do* in life from *who* you are. Separate the person from the actions. You know this is a powerful concept when sales trainers, ministers, and motivational gurus are teaching the same message!

Without this separation, salespeople confuse their role performance with their self-worth. When they fail in their role as a salesperson, they take the failure personally. They allow that failure in their role as a seller to affect their feelings of self-worth and importance. Teach and remind your team that when they make a selling mistake, they failed in their role as a seller, their *do*, not their *who*. They ran a lousy sales call. Period.

Don't Confuse Your Do with Your Who

It's great to teach this concept; however, I will give you a warning. Salespeople don't embrace or own this concept overnight. Like any good habit or skill, it must be revisited and practiced. Your sales team has been conditioned that their performance in their sales role equals their self-worth. It's the reason we have titles on business cards. My role, my title, tells others my level of importance in the world. I've yet to see a business card that states: honest, compassionate, and loyal human being.

You can spot people who measure their self-worth by their *do* fairly quickly. They are experts at name-dropping, telling you about their fourth home and their W-2 earnings. Their role as a successful businessperson defines their inner feelings of self-worth. I remember meeting a consultant and was fascinated by how quickly he was able to inform people about his villa in Italy. "Oh, you like coffee. My villa in Italy has a great coffee maker." His *who* was definitely defined by his *do*.

When conducting coaching sessions, incorporate language to remind your salespeople to take your feedback on their *do*, their role as a salesperson, not their *who*, their self-worth. It can be as simple as saying, "I want to give you some feedback and also want to remind you that my intent in giving this feedback is to make you better in your role as a seller. Please take this feedback, this coaching, on your performance as a salesperson, your *do* not your *who*." Gain agreement on this concept and create a better coaching environment to give well-intended and important feedback. Help your sales team fail well, fail fast, and move forward.

Develop a salesperson's *who*, their inner confidence. The result is a sales team that bounces back from setbacks and is comfortable with continuous evaluation of skills and attitudes. As Reverend Bacon, well-known faith leader, once said, "We make mistakes but we are not mistakes."

Get Fierce about Learning the Lesson

Like most salespeople, I am competitive. I have failed as much as I have won. Over the years, I have learned to use my competitiveness to embrace failure for good. Because if I am going to fail, I'm fierce about learning as many lessons as I can from the failure.

Here's a great exercise to help your sales team move beyond the rhetoric and motivational speeches around failing. Help your team discover for themselves how failure really does help them win more business.

Slow your fast-moving sales team down and have them apply the EQ skill of self-awareness. Help them discover *and* believe the priceless lessons gained from trying, risking, and sometimes failing.

This exercise helps your sales team see the reality of life and sales. We'd all like to succeed at everything we try. The reality is, sometimes a person just can't learn something until they've failed at something.

Fierce Lessons Exercise

1. Have each person on your sales team write down a failure they've experienced in business or sales.
2. Ask them to answer this question. "Did you fail in your role, your *do*, or your *who*?"
3. Next, have your team write down at least three lessons learned from the failure.
4. Have them circle the lessons they could have learned without the failure *or* learned as quickly without the failure.
5. Ask your team to describe specifically how the lessons learned have positively affected future sales calls. What did they do better? What selling mistakes did they avoid?

I have conducted this exercise hundreds of times and each time I hear mini epiphanies. Salespeople finally believe they learn more from failures than successes. It's no longer just a cute motivational quote on the wall.

As you facilitate this important topic, ask your sales team to do some math. Ten lessons learned from each failure multiplied by ten failures equals a hundred lessons. Salespeople who are willing to risk, fail, and learn are likely to be a hundred times smarter than their competitors!

Incorporate lessons-learned language into daily and weekly sales conversations. With any type of setback, adversity, or failure, ask, "What's the lesson learned? How will this lesson serve you moving forward?"

Nelson Mandela, the late great leader and revolutionary, said, "I never lose. I either win or I learn." A great quote for all of us to teach our sales teams.

Reframe Failure

I was floundering my first year in this business of selling sales and sales management training. You think your prospects are tough. Try selling speaking and sales training services to the best sales-people in the world—CEOs and VPs of sales. Not an easy sale.

One of my early mentors noted my frustration, rising stress, and self-doubt. He strengthened my bounce-back muscle by changing my perspective. Instead of giving me several rah-rah, "Atta girl" speeches, he reframed my thinking. His advice was to get to a hundred noes from prospects as fast as I could. Now, that was a goal I was certain I could achieve! He shared: "By the time you've heard a hundred noes, you will have heard every question or objection possible in selling sales and sales management training."

That advice was such a gift. My mentor showed me how to fail well, fail fast, and learn the lessons. He was right. By the time I had received a hundred rejections (yes, I achieved my goal), I was on my way to earning a hundred yeses.

Did You Fail Today?

Sara Blakely, founder of SPANX, is the youngest woman to join the *Forbes* world billionaires list without the help of a husband or inheritance. Her story is a classic one of working through failures and setbacks.

At age twenty-seven, Blakely moved to Atlanta and set aside her entire $5,000 savings to start a hosiery company. She cold-called on hosiery mills to make a prototype, only to be repeatedly told no. Finally, she received a call back from a hosiery factory in Asheboro, North Carolina, where she'd initially been turned away. The manager had two daughters and shared Blakely's hosiery product, nylons without feet. They loved it and he agreed to manufacture her innovative product. What kept Blakely going in the face of so many "not interested" responses? Sara gives credit to her father. Growing up, her father would ask Sara and her brother the same question during dinner: "What have you failed at this week?" In several interviews she has shared, "My dad growing up encouraged me and my brother to fail. The gift he was giving me is that failure is not trying versus the outcome. It's really allowed me to be much freer in trying things and spreading my wings in life."

Sales managers, move beyond motivational rhetoric and add one more coaching question to your coaching toolbox. "What did you fail at today? This week?" Make failing and risk-taking part of your sales team's selling process and journey to improvement.

Normalize Failure

I was asked to participate on a panel for our local National Speakers Association chapter a few years ago. The panel was comprised of successful, veteran speakers addressing a group of aspiring speakers. The moderator asked us to share a failure story from building our businesses. It was a great question and the stories shared were hilarious and ended up serving two purposes:

- Aspiring speakers heard stories of failures from what looked like a group of polished, never-had-a-problem, seasoned speakers. One speaker shared her story of falling off the stage right in the middle of a keynote. (I'm not making this up.) These stories of failure provided hope. "Heck, if these speakers can do it, maybe I can as well."

- The stories gave the audience proof that repeated failures didn't destroy our careers or self-worth. We all lived to tell our stories and lived to establish thriving businesses.

The Story behind the Glory

I was working with a group of bright, young financial planners. During my pre-event interviews, I interviewed one of their rising stars. This young man had me laughing as he shared the many sales activities he attempted to grow his book of business. Early morning breakfast meetings, after-work networking, cold calls, sponsoring events. Many were a waste of time and money, but to his credit he persevered. With his permission, I shared his stories of failing with the group. One young woman was listening intently and raised her hand. "So, what I'm hearing is that we often see the glory but we don't see the story."

She got it. Salespeople often see the glory but don't know the story. They see a successful salesperson who seems to make his numbers with ease and no effort. What they don't see or hear about is the fifty noes Mr. Success heard before receiving his first yes. Salespeople see their colleague and great speaker. What they don't see is the salesperson putting in the time to attend Toastmasters because she bombed several big-time sales presentations.

Normalize failure in your sales organization. During your group sales meetings, ask members of the team to share stories of risk, failure, and lessons learned. Their stories normalize failure and help fellow team members recognize that failing is just part of the journey to becoming exceptional.

Make sure your sales team learns the story behind the glory.

Sales Leaders EQ Action Plan

1. Work on the right end of the sales performance issue. Does your salesperson lack selling skills or is fear of failure inhibiting the execution of selling skills?
2. Teach your sales team the power of separating their *do* from their *who*. Incorporate this language into your coaching conversations.
3. Create a lessons-learned sales culture. Get fierce about the lessons gained from failure.
4. Reward and reframe failure. "What did you fail at today?"
5. Normalize failure.

15

Stress, Sales, Success, and Satisfaction

MEET JULIA. SHE'S BEEN a top sales producer for fifteen years and is a person who is described as perpetually upbeat and positive. But lately, her sales results have been inconsistent, hitting quota one month, not the next month. She is short with colleagues and other members of the team.

Julia is struggling. She's managing a lot of stress in her personal and professional life. She's a member of the sandwich generation. Her aging parents are resisting moving into assisted living, so much of Julia's free time is spent helping them. Julia's two children are teenagers and have become experts at pushing her hot buttons on a daily basis.

On the professional front, achieving sales results is getting tougher. An aggressive new competitor has entered her territory and is lowballing prices. She is experiencing more and more prospects defaulting to status quo simply because they are overwhelmed. Sticking with the status quo is easier than making a decision to move their business. Oh, and the big deal that was supposed to close—not happening. The prospect just announced they are being sold.

Let's add one more factor to complete this scenario. The company is rolling out a new ERP system and the rollout is not going well. Customers are upset with incorrect invoices and installments. Julia is tired, demotivated, and sick days are increasing.

Her concerned sales manager provides Julia with more coaching around lead generation, pipeline management, objection handling, questioning skills, selling value not price, but sees little or no improvement. Why? Because the sales manager is working on the wrong end of the problem. Julia may need more coaching around her selling skills and approach. But she also needs help managing stress.

According to a HubSpot study, 54 percent of salespeople describe their life as stressful and 68 percent as challenging. Stress causes burnout and turnover as high as 27 percent, double the rate in the general workforce.

Burnout is now included in the eleventh revision of the International Classification of Diseases (ICD-11) as an occupational phenomenon. It is defined as a syndrome conceptualized as resulting from chronic workplace stress that has not been successfully managed.

Stress costs sales organizations a lot of money. Salespeople execute at half-speed because they are fatigued. Peak performance is never reached because peak performance takes energy and a positive outlook. As a result, salespeople deliver below-average efforts and below-average sales results.

Great Selling Is a Combination of Psychology, Physiology, and Consultative Selling Skills

In our Emotional Intelligence for Sales Success workshops, we teach that effective sales—and sales management—requires an understanding of psychology, physiology, and consultative selling skills. Most sales managers and salespeople aren't aware of how physiology affects their ability to consistently execute the right selling behaviors.

Let's go back to the paper-rock-scissors game. Rock is your body's physiology. Scissors is a person's selling skills. When a salesperson is stressed, the body's physiological reaction to stress will smash or at least blunt a salesperson's ability to effectively apply sales knowledge and skills.

When a salesperson is stressed, the body releases the stress hormone cortisol. Too much cortisol creates fatigue, depression, lack of sleep, and lack of creativity. In a study of more than two thousand people, participants with the highest levels of cortisol performed worse on tests of memory, organization, visual perception, and attention. Obviously, not a winning formula for achieving sustainable sales results.

Stress Management Is Sales Management

Stress is a part of life, and the better you can equip your sales team to understand and manage it, the better chance you have of managing a sales team that hits the sales quota and the fun quota.

Apply self-awareness and think about times you've felt stress. Were you operating at your best? One of the common emotions causing stress is that of feeling out of control. Apply empathy and step into your salesperson's shoes and tune into the selling scenarios where they are feeling out of control:

- Every prospect and customer in a salesperson's territory is demanding information or deliverables in the same week. The salesperson's calendar is overbooked and out of control. *Stress.*
- The operations side of the business isn't keeping up with the sales generated by the sales organization. The salesperson is fielding angry calls from customers asking about their orders. Operations doesn't report to sales so the salesperson feels out of control in trying to correct the situation. *Stress.*
- The company has rolled out a new CRM system and the deadline is looming to integrate into daily sales processes.

The salesperson is feeling the pressure to master the new system and feels out of control. *Stress.*

- The accounting department screws up invoicing and the salesperson's *large* new client threatens to take away the business. Accounting is buried, trying to keep up with the company's growth. No one is returning the salesperson's phone calls or emails so he can't get answers to his customers. The salesperson feels out of control. *Stress.*
- Your industry is being disrupted. The salesperson must amp up her learning to remain relevant. She's wondering how she can tackle all the new information coming at her each week. She feels out of control. *Stress.*

Stress isn't going away but sales managers can improve their sales team's ability to manage it.

Building Your Sales Team's Stress Muscles

Developing your sales team's ability to manage stress is like developing any skill. Sales managers must first pay attention and devote time and education to developing their sales team's stress muscle.

Revisit chapter five and teach your sales team the concepts around internal and external locus of control. Internal locus of control (increased control) equals decreased stress. Decreased stress equals increased energy, improved problem-solving skills, and happiness.

Author Scott Halford summarizes the difference in internal and external locus of control nicely in his book *Activate Your Brain*.

When you feel that sense of control over what happens to you, you're more likely to be successful. You'll take responsibility for the ups and downs that come your way—a not-so-secret to success. Being aware of what we can control puts us in the driver's seat. You can start moving toward an internal locus of control simply by listening to the way you speak. When something occurs that isn't to your liking, if your immediate response is to look for all the reasons why other people or circumstances cause this bad thing in your life, take a moment before responding and reframe the statement into an "I" statement. What did you have to do with the scenario? What could you have done to change the outcome? That's taking control. When we switch our language, we open up our brain to the possibility of learning from a mistake.

Open up your sales team's brains on new ways to take control and change their existing circumstances. Include stress management coaching in your individual or group meetings. Remind your sales team about the impact of the reptilian brain on logical and rational thinking. The reptilian brain is wired for survival, and when stress appears, it raises the red flag of fear, flapping loudly. Fear is the great paralyzer of action, and action is needed to take control and reduce stress. The reptilian brain works overtime trying to get a salesperson to focus and worry about everything out of his control!

Help your salesperson engage the logical part of his brain to regain a sense of control. Ask your salesperson to write down all the areas of sales that he can control, regardless of external circumstances. Here are a few suggestions to get the "take control" coaching conversation started.

Control What You Can Control

- **Sales activity.** Salespeople are in control of doing the work. Make five more prospecting outreaches. Come in early and don't go home until you've set two appointments. Connect with potential referral partners, ask clients for referrals, become active in your trade association, host an event with one of your strategic partners, conduct a provocative webinar. **Sales activity is in a salesperson's control.**

- **Sales skills.** Salespeople are in control of learning and practicing new selling skills. That low-price competitor can be beaten by learning new skills and strategies around selling value. A salesperson can target better prospects, ones that still pay for value. Salespeople can ask their sales manager for advice. A salesperson can call a colleague to practice. **Improving selling skills is in a salesperson's control.**

- **Sales attitude.** Salespeople are in control of their mindsets. They control what time they go to bed so they can wake up early, allowing time for introspection. Each morning, salespeople have the ability to start the day with gratitude, writing down three to five things for which they are grateful. This habit triggers the reward center of the brain, releasing the feel-good hormone dopamine, which is much better than the stress hormone cortisol. They control the company they keep. They can choose to hang out with salespeople who are walking around glasses that are always full, not half-empty. **Attitude is in a salesperson's control.**

- **Sales and service.** The company is experiencing service issues and the salesperson is flooded with complaints. A salesperson may not be in charge of operations but they are in charge of returning calls, giving clients bad news, and not dodging the tough conversations. Customers don't like mistakes but they really dislike salespeople who don't call, own up to the problems, or keep them apprised of steps to fix problems. **Salespeople can control giving exceptional customer service.**

Teach your sales team to focus on what they can control instead of what's out of their control. Increased control results in decreased stress.

In my early years of learning the sales training and speaking business, I conducted practice sales calls. I'd set appointments with prospects that didn't fit my ideal profile, ones from whom I was probably going to hear no. Why? I created a safe environment to practice and try new skills. Even if the sales call didn't result in a close, I observed how my questions landed, learned about potential objections, all of which helped me get better at my craft. I was in control of my sales development.

No Victims Allowed

If you've been in sales long enough, you've walked out of an appointment or hung up the phone with a prospect and said, "Now, that really sucked." Pessimism, self-doubt, and victim mentality show up in full force. "I have the worst prospects—no one can sell to these people." This out-of-control thinking leads to increased stress and a victim mentality.

Teach your sales team to stop complaining about tough prospects. Be grateful for tough prospects because they are a salesperson's best teacher. I've had more than one tough prospect elevate my selling skills, making me a better sales professional. Those tough prospects asked more questions, pointed questions, and better questions. They made me work harder to get better at my profession. Tough prospects aren't always pleasant calls; however, with the right perspective, they always provide a free sales education.

Work with your sales team and apply the EQ skills of self-awareness and self-regard. They must have the awareness and confidence to understand where they can do better on a sales call, what they can control.

Teach and coach your salesperson to ask himself introspective questions, ones that reduce stress, increase ownership, and elevate optimism.

- What part of this do I need to own? Did I prepare enough for this appointment or am I starting to slip into a little bit of complacency?
- What did I learn from this appointment? How will the new learning help me do better on future sales calls?
- What did I do well? How can I bring more of those skills to every sales conversation?
- Who can I reach out to in my network that can provide me with additional insights?

Change your salesperson's self-talk from that of a victim to that of a victor. Teach and remind salespeople they are not victims of their circumstances; they are in control of their circumstances. They are victors, ones who have the control to take the right actions to continually improve and succeed.

Be Thankful for Tough Prospects

Here's a great exercise to conduct with your sales team. It helps them recognize the power of gratitude, control, and optimism. Have them craft a letter to a difficult prospect.

Dear Ms./Mr. Prospect:

Thanks for meeting with me this week. Your good questions and thought-provoking questions made me realize my selling tools are in need of serious sharpening.

I could have better prepared for the meeting as the questions you asked and objections you raised aren't new. However, without preparation, I stumbled on answers—which probably raised concerns in your mind about my company's credibility and ability to execute.

Thanks for reminding me that I might be getting complacent. In this day and age of information, there is no reason not to be prepared for a sales meeting. If I had been better prepared, perhaps the meeting would have been more relevant for you and a second meeting would be on the calendar.

Thanks again for being a tough prospect. I will reach out next week and admit my less-than-perfect sales performance. If you give me another opportunity, I will show up prepared and ready to add value.

Sincerely,
The Self-Aware, Grateful, Take-Control, Optimistic Salesperson

Lighten Up

Optimistic salespeople are similar to great comedians in that comedians actually love running into situations that often create stress for other people. Why? It's new material!

I learned this stress management tool from my colleagues in the speaking business who are humorists. These are some of the funniest people on the planet, and not surprisingly, they are often less stressed than most of us.

I was listening to a panel of humorists during one of our local Colorado National Speakers Association meetings. This funny group of speakers was trying to teach the rest of us (who may need to work a little harder at finding the humor) the methodology for developing our humor bones. It became obvious to me that comedians and humorists view the world through an entirely different lens than most of us. They see stressful events as gifts because these events are their future funny stories for their next engagement.

My colleague Karyn Ruth White is a laugh-out-loud keynote speaker and comedian, who teaches companies how to manage stress and laugh more. She shared a story that is a classic example of viewing a stressful situation through a humorous lens.

Late one night, Karyn Ruth was checking into a historic hotel in Colorado. There was no bellman to be found, just her and the young lady at registration. Karyn Ruth got her room key and started down the long hall, hauling her own luggage. Cranky, she opened her hotel room door and flipped on the lights. What she saw was a room filled with fleas! The hotel was undergoing renovation and apparently the displaced fleas had decided to meet in her room.

Karyn Ruth shared with the audience how she was tempted to march back down that long hall and give the registration clerk a piece of her mind. But rather than default to a stress response, she asked herself this question, "Is there anything funny about this?" So, she approached the young lady behind the counter and said, "We need to chat about my room. I could have sworn I asked for a single occupancy." Alarmed, the clerk asked, "Is there someone in your room, Miss White?" Karyn Ruth's response, "No, there's not *someone* in my room, there is a party going on in there . . . thousands of tiny sand fleas doing the Macarena, drinking little tropical drinks with itsy bitsy umbrellas in them, and I'm pretty sure there's a group in the corner . . . smokin' something!"

After a moment of shock, the registration clerk realized that Karyn Ruth was making light of the situation and she laughed along. She apologized and gave Karyn Ruth an upgrade to one of their best suites at no charge and a gift certificate for a free weekend for two.

As Karyn Ruth was checking out, the same young lady at registration asked her, "Miss White, has anyone ever told you that they really like the way you complain?"

This panel of humorists gave all of the participants great tools for managing stress. Lighten up! See adversity through a new lens: a new avenue for providing great stories to share in trainings and keynotes. That perspective keeps me happy and lowers my stress.

Humor Management Is Stress Management

Teach your sales team the power of using humor to decrease stress and improve their optimism. When your sales team experiences a failure, setback, or adversity, ask your sales team to immediately shift their thinking by asking these questions:

- What's funny about this?
- Where's the humor in this situation?
- What kind of story do I have to tell?

After attending our Ei Sales Management Course, one of our clients asked everyone to come to the next sales meeting, prepared with their worst sales war story.

The stories were hysterical. The best one came from a new business development person. This young man is dedicated and really good about doing the work necessary to fill the sales pipeline. He shared his story of foot canvassing an office building. (Which is a prospecting activity that works in their industry.) One of the tenants in the building didn't like this approach and asked him to leave the building. Being a tenacious young salesperson, he kept foot canvassing. At the end of a lot of door knocking, he entered the elevator on the twentieth floor, and unfortunately for him, he ended up standing by the tenant who had asked him to leave.

For twenty floors, he heard comments about people showing up unwanted in the building. It was the longest elevator ride of his life. His optimistic note to his peers: take the stairs.

Sales Leaders EQ Action Plan

1. Make a decision to teach your sales team key principles of stress management. Stress management is sales management.
2. Help your sales team focus on what they can control, not what is out of their control.
3. Teach the power of perspective and optimism.
4. Have your sales team write a letter to their toughest prospect.
5. Include a humor section in your next sales meeting about the worst sales call. Hold a contest for the funniest story!

16

Focus: Be Here Now

BOB FLEXON, FORMER CEO of Dynegy, was on a mission to change the culture at his company. He arrived at Dynegy four months before they filed for bankruptcy. Under his leadership, Mr. Flexon implemented changes designed to change the culture. His belief: change the culture and you will change revenues and achieve long-term success.

Of the many changes he made, one was his focus on being present and in the moment. Dynegy employees were banned from checking email and phones during meetings. (What a concept. People actually paying attention to each other and what is being said during a meeting.) He installed "culture champions" to reinforce the message. When they saw a colleague checking their phone, they'd call out the behavior and announce, "Jennifer, be here now."

Fear of Missing Out

"FOMO"—fear of missing out—is alive and well in corporate America. Everyone wants to be everywhere but where they are.

And too many sales managers are settling for lousy business etiquette, allowing salespeople to be half-present when engaged in conversations. The last time I checked, being half-present isn't a great selling habit to bring into a high-level sales conversation. That which we do repeatedly becomes a habit, and like it or not, this habit will show up during a sales meeting.

A well-run consultative sales meeting ranges from one to two hours. These meetings require extreme focus from salespeople as they ask questions and listen closely to the answers. But here's the problem: a salesperson with poor focus skills has difficulty conducting an hour-long sales meeting because they've never focused that long before the sales meeting! Their brain starts wandering after twenty minutes so they miss half the conversation. The habit of focus must be developed *before* conducting a sales meeting because a salesperson can't apply a habit that has not been developed.

"But, Colleen, you don't understand. Attention spans are decreasing." Blah, blah, blah. How many of you would accept that excuse from a surgeon? "Mr. Patient, just giving you a heads-up. I'll need to step away from surgery every twenty minutes to gather my thoughts. Sorry about that. You know, everyone has a short attention span."

We can do better.

Love the One You're With

A couple of years ago, I met with a marketing consultant. The purpose and objective of the meeting was to learn more about each other and determine if there was a good fit in the services she offered and the services we needed. Upon sitting down, she immediately set her smartphone on the table. Dumb move because her actions immediately clued me in that she had not engaged in pre-call planning, since this is a topic I teach, rant, and write about. The real kicker was when the phone vibrated and, mid-sentence, she interrupted our conversation to look at the incoming message. Yup, I was meeting with Pavlov's dog, and I certainly wasn't feeling the love. Let's just say there wasn't a second meeting.

Leading in a FOMO World

I feel your pain as focus is a new challenge for sales leaders to contend with and teach.

Today's sales leaders are charged with developing salespeople in a very distracted world. Twenty years ago, the world wasn't as full of shiny objects. You could actually watch a TV show without ads popping up on the lower left screen! In one second, there are:

- 54,907 Google searches
- 7,252 tweets
- 125,406 YouTube video views
- 2,501,018 emails sent

CEOs, sales managers and salespeople like to disguise the habit of distraction by calling it multitasking. Many people claim to have mastered this skill. What you or your salesperson have mastered is multi-averaging. You're masterful at doing average work and sadly, accepting average work. The research is pretty clear. When an individual engages in multitasking, the accuracy and quality of the work decreases. It's called dual-task interference.

Go to a soccer field, basketball court, or football field. Have you ever seen an athlete practicing the game playbook stop and check his or her cell phone and resume practice? *No!*

But I have seen salespeople (and sales managers) practicing a play from the company sales playbook, stop, check their cell phones, and resume training.

Who do you think will achieve the highest level of mastery? The athlete or the salesperson?

I'm putting my money on the athlete.

Focus, Learning, and Revenues

The battle cry from sales managers, salespeople, and sales gurus is that prospects are more educated and expect more from a salesperson. So what? Salespeople have access to more information and tools than ever before to be successful in life. Quit whining about increasing demands from prospects and customers. Develop your sales team skills to meet the demands. One of the most important skills that the sales force of the future needs is the ability to learn, unlearn, and relearn because business and sales will continue to change and evolve. The internet wasn't even in existence when I started in sales!

But here's the challenge. Focus is necessary for salespeople to learn new skills. Distractions are the enemy of greatness. David Rock, author of *Your Brain at Work*, provides great insights around this topic. He explains:

> Understanding a new idea involves creating maps in the prefrontal cortex that represent new, incoming information, and connecting these maps to existing maps in the rest of the brain. Making a decision involves activating a series of maps in the prefrontal cortex and making a choice between these maps.

Reread that paragraph. Still think you can manage distractions, multitask, and improve critical thinking skills or selling skills?

Sorry—until the robots take over, you and your sales team will need to abide by the brain's rules for learning.

Stop accepting excuses and start expecting excellence. Everyone can improve their ability to focus—and it starts with your leadership. Daniel Goleman wrote an entire book around this topic titled *Focus*. He shares, "Cognitive efforts like learning require active attention." It's your job to teach and model focus and paying attention so your sales team can learn, unlearn, and relearn new skills and knowledge.

Focus, Attention, and Empathy

As discussed in chapter twelve, empathy is a powerful selling skill. It requires paying attention to all the conversations occurring in the room, both the spoken and unspoken conversations. But in order for a salesperson to be able to pay attention and demonstrate empathy, they must first be able to focus. Focus precedes attention and attention precedes empathy.

The twenty-first-century habit of immediately checking anything that beeps, lights up, or vibrates is a habit that decreases a person's ability to focus. Decreased focus leads to decreased attention—which leads to decreased empathy.

Is anyone seeing a problem with this chicken and egg pattern occurring in sales?

I hope it's becoming clear how lack of focus affects learning selling skills, the quality of sales conversations, and sales results.

Sales managers, if you really believe that paying attention, being present, and demonstrating empathy is important for conducting effective sales meetings, teach and model the importance of focus to your sales team. Create tech-free meetings and conversations. Salespeople with the attention span of a gnat aren't going to create consistent sales results for your sales organization.

Be here now.

Focus and Productivity

As you will learn in the next chapter, productivity experts teach the value of calendar blocking to better manage your day. The Franklin Covey organization stresses the importance of working on the important and not urgent tasks. Sales gurus teach and preach the importance of pre-call planning and preparation to make sure you are showing up as a value-added salesperson.

But here's the problem. The above strategies work, but they only work if a salesperson has the ability to focus. These proven strategies for productivity and success require a person's attention and cognitive skills.

Salespeople can waste up to twenty hours a month because of their inability to focus. Let's do some quick math. One hour wasted each day due to lack of focus multiplied by five days a week multiplied by four weeks equals twenty hours of wasted time in one month. If you manage a sales team of ten, you're looking at two hundred hours. That's valuable time that could have been invested in acquiring and retaining clients!

Effective salespeople are focused salespeople. They consistently:

- **Calendar block**—they know what they are going to focus on and accomplish during specific times of the day.
- **Focus on accomplishing similar tasks**—like prospecting, client review meetings, creating proposals, and entering data into CRM systems. They know moving from one task to another is not efficient or effective. Research shows that when people flit from one task to another, it can take as long as twenty-three minutes to get back on task. That's a lot of wasted time.
- **Manage their technology**—rather letting their technology manage them. A study by Kleiner, Perkins, Caufield, and Byer found that the average person

checks their phone 150 times a day. And we wonder why salespeople aren't achieving quota? The unfocused salesperson spends all day checking messages rather than taking action and achieving sales results.

Mr. Flexon understood the power of focus. While CEO of Dynegy, he had a mounted plaque underneath his computer monitor that stated, "Be Here Now." A good strategy for all of us striving to be better sales leaders.

Sales Leaders EQ Action Plan

1. Make a decision. Accept the new challenge of sales leadership, one requiring you to teach and model the discipline of focus.
2. Identify areas where FOMO is getting in the way of your sales team achieving results.
3. Teach and model focus during your one-on-one meetings and group sales meetings. Create tech-free zones.
4. Stop believing you can't do anything to improve attention spans. Become part of the "we can do better" movement.
5. Create your own poster that states: Be Here Now.

17

It's Time to Teach Time Management

I WAS FORTUNATE BECAUSE my first exposure to time management principles occurred in my twenties. My employer sent me to a time-management training course with a great instructor. I still remember a metaphor she used in teaching participants how to tackle big projects. She called it the Swiss cheese method.

Many of us avoid tackling the big projects, the ones with high payoff, because big projects look like a big block of cheese. You can't eat this piece of cheese, or tackle a big project, at one seating. (Unless you've had a really bad day . . .) Her suggestion was to poke holes in big projects, make a big daunting task look like Swiss cheese. It was a great example of how to break down big projects into bite-size pieces.

Because of that early exposure to the value of time management, I've always taught simple principles of productivity to my sales teams. Time is finite. It levels the playing field because all salespeople get the same twenty-four hours in a day. Wise salespeople who learn good productivity habits use their time wisely.

I've heard more than one sales manager or salesperson proclaim that salespeople are disorganized—it's just their nature. Sorry but I'm not buying that sales myth.

My anecdotal research suggests otherwise. My observation, in working with hundreds of top sales performers, is that really good salespeople possess great time management skills. They are masters at managing their calendars rather than the calendar managing them. That's how and why they accomplish so much without stressing out and burning out.

Now you might be thinking. *What—teach time management? I am a sales manager. My job is to educate my sales team on sales strategy and tactics. My "time" needs to be devoted to teaching my team how to fill the sales pipeline, run effective sales meetings, and close business.*

Good luck with that thinking. Salespeople with poor time management skills don't have time to apply your great coaching. They tend to operate in what the late Stephen Covey coined as the "tyranny of the urgent." They spend all their time in instant-gratification activities that often produce below-average results. They don't have time to:

- *Execute a consistent sales activity plan*, because there is no proactive time blocked on their calendar. Prospecting efforts are sporadic and sales results unpredictable.

- *Master selling skills.* Mastery requires proactively setting aside time to practice.

- *Be creative.* They are always busy putting out fires instead of thinking of ways to prevent repeatable fires.

I've coached hundreds of sales calls and it became evident to me many years ago that lack of time management skills is one of the reasons for poor sales results. Think of time management as priority management. Without it, many salespeople never get to their most important priority, which is called selling!

Time Management and Delayed Gratification

Salespeople with poor time management skills are stressed-out salespeople. As covered in the previous chapters, prolonged stress causes the body to produce cortisol, creating fatigue, lack of creativity—and ultimately lack of motivation. You can preach and teach sales all you want. But tired salespeople aren't your most effective salespeople. The body always wins.

Salespeople with poor time management skills unknowingly fall prey to the busy-but-not-productive syndrome. You've managed this salesperson. She is a hard worker, always busy. This salesperson is no slouch. The problem is that this salesperson works *harder*, not smarter.

This salesperson operates in the instant gratification bucket, giving into the pull of what is easy. She constantly reacts to the latest distraction or request.

Instant gratification salespeople are busy responding immediately to emails and phone calls, prospecting, writing proposals, running sales meetings, and firefighting. But many of these same activities would create better sales results if salespeople invested more time in the delayed gratification bucket.

Consistent sales results happen when salespeople invest time in delayed gratification activities such as pre-call planning, studying, practicing selling skills, creating compelling value propositions, investing time with potential referral partners, as well as putting in systems and processes to prevent repeatable fires.

The challenge for sales managers and salespeople is that delayed gratification activities don't have a pressing deadline. There is no urgency in finding time to execute these activities. But it's the sales chicken-and-egg scenario again. When salespeople don't invest time in delayed gratification activities, they fall into the trap of working harder, not smarter.

Take a look at the chart on the next pages and think about areas where your sales team is falling into the busy, not productive trap.

Salespeople with an Instant Gratification Mindset	Salespeople with a Delayed Gratification Mindset
Prospecting Calls and Outreaches	**Prospecting Calls and Outreaches**
Not effective because the salesperson didn't invest time in analyzing whether or not this prospect fits the company ideal client profile. Keeps meeting with prospects who can't or won't buy.	Effective because there was time invested to determine if this prospect fit the company's ideal client profile. Achieves sales results because they are meeting with the right targets.
Prospecting outreaches are deleted because they look and sound like every other salesperson. They're really busy reaching out to prospects with canned, generic, and nonrelevant value propositions.	Connect with prospects because they invested time in crafting prospecting messages customized for the buyer, industry, competitor gap, and pain point. They avoid one-size-fits-all value propositions.
Referral Partner Meetings with Non-Competing Vendors	**Referral Partner Meetings with Non-Competing Vendors**
Not effective. The salesperson keeps meeting with potential partners that can't or won't refer the right type of business.	Effective because the salesperson designed qualifying questions to determine if this potential partner can/will refer business. Questions such as:
Your salesperson's coffee partner doesn't call on the C-suite. Keeps referring your salesperson to non-decision makers.	Who and what level is their potential partner calling on?
The salesperson's coffee partner wins business on low price so only gives referrals to cheap, transactional prospects.	Does this person sell on value or price?
The salesperson's referral partner is treated like a vendor, not a partner, by their clients.	What is their relationship with their clients?
Your salesperson receives the same treatment when given an introduction.	Are they treated as a partner or a vendor?
Your salesperson's coffee partner doesn't embrace the power of reciprocation. They are a taker, not a giver.	Are they a giver or taker?

(cont.)

Salespeople with an Instant Gratification Mindset	Salespeople with a Delayed Gratification Mindset
Multitasking	Multitasking
Salesperson is checking email every five minutes or each time an alert pops up.	Productive salespeople don't! They're effective because phone/email alerts are turned off.
Never completes intentional work or focused work. And if they do, there are mistakes and rework. Completed work is average at best.	They focus on one sales task at a time, completing the task in less time and the completed work is high-quality work.
Conducting Sales Meetings with Prospects and Customers	Conducting Sales Meetings with Prospects and Customers
Ineffective because the salesperson didn't take the time to engage in pre-call planning. He is winging the sales conversation rather than mastering and leading an effective conversation.	Effective because the salesperson took the time to pre-call plan. Compelling questions are developed and asked during the sales meeting.
He didn't plan for objections so ends up defending and justifying, sending prospects into fight or flight responses.	Didn't get stumped by objections because the salesperson created a strategy for preempting or handling.
Blows the call in the first five minutes because she didn't adjust her communication style to match the prospect's style.	The salesperson identified the prospect's personality style and adapts her approach to create rapport and trust.

Stop the Madness

It's easy for sales managers and salespeople to default to an instant gratification mindset. Blame it on your reptilian brain. Without self-awareness, this illogical part of your brain will ambush your day and calendar.

When the reptilian brain sees a bunch of emails piling up, it shouts, "Danger, danger . . . you are missing out on something.

Danger, danger, you will never get caught up" (even though more than half of the messages can wait for a response or don't deserve your attention at all).

There are great productivity experts out there, and I encourage you to hire them. But you can also start with some very basic time management principles that will make an immediate difference for your team. Time is finite and so is energy. These ideas will help your sales team maximize both.

Mind Map Your Way to Sales Success

I feel sorry for salespeople who haven't been taught the basics of calendar blocking because it is a game changer. Without education, many salespeople mistakenly think that logging appointments and prospecting time on the calendar is enough. It's not. Salespeople need to calendar block prep time, follow-up time, and white space time. You've heard the expression "the devil is in the details." And this is really applicable when planning your week or month.

One of the best tools I use for calendar management is mind mapping. We teach this process in our sales management courses and it's always a hit. Mind mapping is powerful because a salesperson can translate what is in his mind to a visual picture. The brain likes and understands pictures, so using this technique allows salespeople to organize information faster and better.

Include this mind mapping exercise at your next sales meeting. Warning, this is not a quick exercise, and you will be tempted to shortcut the process. Check your delayed gratification skills and put in the time to walk your sales team through the multiple steps. Adults learn by doing and mind mapping is one of those tools you can't learn by hearing how to do it.

The reward is seeing your salespeople gain an understanding of why they aren't getting everything done or why they are working long hours and still not achieving goals. See the steps in Figure 17.1.

MIND MAP

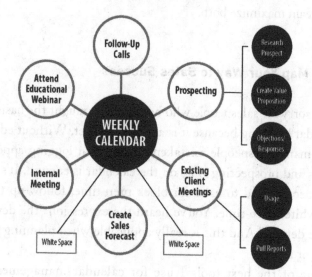

FIGURE 17.1

1. Give each person on your team a large piece of flip chart paper. Have each salesperson draw a circle in the middle of the paper with the words "weekly calendar" written in the middle. (As they master this technique, they can move to a "monthly calendar.")

2. Next, have each salesperson write down everything that needs to be accomplished that week. Have them create random circles around the main circle. The circles might include prospecting outreaches, sales meetings, existing client calls/meetings, creating a pursuit strategy for new

prospects, account management review meetings, forecasting, and internal meetings.

3. Once the random circles are established, have each salesperson create branches off of the various circles to capture all the details that need to be completed in order to accomplish the specific task or sales activity. For example, a salesperson calendar blocks one hour for conducting a new prospect appointment. What she often doesn't calendar block is:

> *Time to research the prospect.*
> *Time to research the prospect's existing vendor.*
> *Time to create a customized value proposition to open up a consultative sales call.*
> *Time to identify and think through potential objections and craft responses.*

An existing client meeting circle might have branches that include:

> *Time to pull reports and analytics of sales.*
> *Time to call the customer service department and check service levels/complaints.*
> *Time to write out a new value proposition for the new line of business that will be introduced during the sales meeting.*

4. Have your team add one more section to their mind map labeled "white space." This square represents time on the calendar where nothing is scheduled. We all know that each day there are unplanned events that need to be dealt with. Salespeople get stressed out and feel their day spiraling out of control because they haven't planned for these events, the predictable issues of business. Stop repeating the same mistake and set aside time to plan for the unplanned.

5. This next step is where the exercise gets interesting. Have each member of your team transfer the details from the flip chart to their calendars. Be prepared to hear complaints because this step takes time, thinking, and moving things around in order to organize and fit sales activities and tasks into their calendars. This step of the calendar blocking process is the commitment step. The salesperson is committing to a specific time on the calendar for completing an activity. No more winging it. They are proactively managing their time.

This type of thinking and planning helps your sales team gain hours back in their weeks. This creates more time for consistent prospecting outreaches and more effective sales meetings. Sales results improve as does your team's happiness. A salesperson with good time management accomplishes more and stresses less.

The Effective Salesperson

Kathy is a top salesperson for a distribution company. Her territory is in the beautiful mountains of Colorado. However, with that beauty comes the added logistics of clients being spread out and at certain times of the year a lot of traffic.

One of the reasons for Kathy's success is her ability to manage her calendar and still provide exceptional service to clients. At the time we worked with the company, it was not set up with a strong sales support function. This resulted in Kathy fielding most of the customers' questions or concerns. I asked her how she managed juggling sales and customer service. Her answer reflected great impulse control and time management skills. "I've learned that most of the questions need an answer but the answer doesn't mean I have to immediately pull over, call customer service, or check my computer. I always ask,

'Can I get back to you at 3:00 p.m. today, when I am back in my office?' The answer 90 percent of the time is yes. That allows me to focus on one thing at a time. I calendar block sales calls up to a certain time each day, then turn my focus to service and account management calls at the end of the day."

Guard the Calendar and Your Impulses

Okay, the salesperson's calendar is looking good. She's captured and mind mapped the many details to run an effective week. Time is proactively blocked off for proactive prospecting.

Then life happens.

Your salesperson has been pursuing a prospect for weeks and finally connects with him. The salesperson does a great job on the exploratory call and asks if she can set a second meeting, a discovery meeting. The prospect agrees and says that he's available on Tuesday at 10:00 a.m. The salesperson looks at her calendar and sees that she has blocked 10:00 a.m. to noon on Tuesday for prospecting. But she is excited about this opportunity and deletes that prospecting time and replaces it with a new appointment. It's the salesperson's lucky day because another prospect returns the salesperson's prospecting outreach and requests a meeting with the salesperson on Thursday at 1:00 p.m. This time was also calendared for prospecting but opportunity is knocking. The salesperson deletes her prospecting time block and schedules the new prospect meeting.

What's wrong with the picture?

The calendar is running the salesperson rather than the other way around. One week of proactive prospecting has just gone out the window. Not because it wasn't blocked on the calendar. It's because the salesperson gave in to instant gratification and low self-control. The salesperson couldn't manage her impulse to jump on a potential opportunity.

I am reading your minds and you are thinking, "Are you crazy? Take the appointment."

Here's the problem. If a salesperson keeps reacting, not honoring her calendar, she'll end up with weeks without proactive prospecting. Inconsistent activity results in a dismal-looking, empty sales pipeline.

Raise your sales team's awareness on impulse control and honoring their calendar. When I teach this concept, salespeople push back—hard.

"You don't understand our business. My prospect wants that specific time and I've been trying to get ahold of this prospect for a month."

Instead of arguing, I apply reality testing by asking a series of questions.

What would you say to a prospect who asked you for a 10:00 a.m. meeting on Tuesday and you already had that time scheduled to meet with your biggest and best client? Would you blow off your best client?

Or, would you respond to the prospect with, "I am sorry . . . I'm booked . . . can we look at another time?" Is the prospect going to get mad and say, "Well, if I can't have that time, I don't want any time at all?"

Light bulb. "Hmm . . . uh . . . no."

What do you think the prospect will say?

Light bulb. "What else do you have available?"

Sales managers, teach your sales team to manage their calendars and impulses. It's important that salespeople recognize times and triggers that lead to unproductive selling behaviors. Role-play with your team on this very concept so they can learn how easy it is to say, "I am booked . . . could we look at another time?"

I run into the same problem in managing my calendar. I have certain days and times of the week blocked specifically for delayed gratification activities such as writing, designing content, and practicing keynotes. Like every other salesperson on the planet, I also get requests to meet at those times. After experiencing too many weeks of an out-of-control calendar, I've learned to manage my impulses and desire to please. I redirect prospects and clients to dates and times on my calendar set aside for proactive selling conversations.

Time is finite and is one of your sales team's most important assets. Every salesperson has the same twenty-four hours in a day. The successful ones know how to get the most out of their twenty-four hours.

Time to Get Up

This topic always creates a flurry of opinion with the night owls defending their schedules of late to bed and late to rise. I'll let you come to your own conclusion, but the research leans toward the early-to-bed and early-to-rise habit. It will make you healthy, wealthy, and wise.

There is more interesting research from author Thomas C. Corley. In his five-year study of 177 self-made millionaires, he found that nearly 50 percent of them woke up at least three hours before their workday actually began. Well-known early risers include Apple CEO Tim Cook who starts his mornings at 3:45 a.m. Pepsi CEO Indra Nooyi is up by 4:00 a.m and in the office by 7:00 a.m. Richard Branson is also part of the 5:00 a.m. club.

Research confirms the brain, specifically the prefrontal cortex, is most active and readily creative immediately following sleep. Your mind is clearest in the morning and your energy is the highest. This is the best time of the day to invest in those delayed gratification sales activities that will grow your sales skills and sales results.

The first hours of the day are a great time for salespeople to engage in creative work such as writing a blog, crafting a series of compelling email messages, thinking of new ways to serve your clients, creating compelling posts for social media, and brainstorming smart questions that make prospects and customers think.

Unfortunately, a lot of salespeople wake up, hit the snooze button a few times, and rush hour begins, leaving no time for downtime. Research from *Harvard Business Review* shows that speed adversely affects creativity and work. We all admire innovation and disruptive ideas, but innovation can't be rushed. If your sales team needs to think more creatively about solutions, it's best accomplished by slowing down and allowing time for deep thinking. Get up!

The club of early risers shares that getting up early allows them time to read and study, helping them become a true trusted advisor. If you desire to build a sales team of thought leaders, make sure you are encouraging habits that lead to the exposure of new thoughts!

Salespeople who delay deep thinking to later in the workday may find it difficult to accomplish this goal. The brain is like any other muscle, and by afternoon the brain has been used in multiple conversations, decisions, internal meetings, and external meetings. It's tired, and a tired brain is not a creative brain.

When I've made the mistake of scheduling deep-thinking work in the afternoon, I've discovered it takes twice as long and the quality of work isn't as good.

This quote from Daniel Kahneman, author of *Thinking Fast and Slow*, nicely summarizes the importance of time management. "Happiness is determined by factors like your health, your family, relationships, and friendships, and above all by feeling that you are in control of how you spend your time."

Teach your sales team effective time management principles that free up their calendars and their brains. Time management is stress management and happiness management. It's time to teach time management.

Sales Leaders EQ Action Plan

1. Identify areas where your sales team is falling into instant gratification activities rather than delayed gratification activities.
2. Carve out time to teach mind mapping at your next sales meeting.
3. Educate your sales team on the importance of self-awareness and impulse control in honoring their calendars. Role-play with your sales team on handling the predictable temptations that derail calendars.
4. Encourage your sales team to win the morning. Get up early and avoid hurried and harried starts to the day.
5. Model the behavior you expect. Are you running your calendar or is your calendar running you?

For more coaching tools and templates, visit www.Emotional IntelligenceForSalesLeadership.com. We have additional exercises and questions for you to incorporate into daily sales conversations with your team.

PART IV

IT'S BACK TO YOU

It is very important to understand that emotional intelligence is not the opposite of intelligence, it is not the triumph of heart over head—it is the unique intersection of both.

—David Caruso

And if the end result is that someone, somewhere winds up believing they can do something out of the ordinary, well, then you've really made it.

—Angela Ahrendts

18

The Sales EQ
and Sales IQ
of Teaching and Coaching

MIRROR, MIRROR, ON THE wall, am I modeling what I am teaching at all? It's a great question for all of us in sales leadership roles to ask ourselves.

I've focused on the importance of teaching your sales team emotional intelligence skills. In the next few chapters, I will turn the focus back to you. Look in the mirror and ask: Am I modeling the emotional intelligence skills I teach?

Quite a few years ago, we were referred to a company that was interested in obtaining EQ coaching for one of their top sales managers. Steven was a classic example of a sales manager who was really good at the mechanics of sales management. He was intelligent and good at holding his sales team accountable to activity metrics and sales results. His sales team was hitting quota *and* they were also starting to hit the doors, leaving the company because of his abrupt and condescending sales management style.

Senior management was looking at the crystal ball and the future didn't look bright for Steven. He was putting up the numbers but his behaviors didn't support the core values of respect and teamwork espoused by the company. This caused many employees to question how serious the company was about these so-called core values. Could they be ignored as long as you were making lots of money for the company?

They didn't hire us for the engagement; however, I couldn't get this young sales manager out of my mind. So much potential there that might not be achieved. Out of curiosity, I reached out a few months later to his boss, asking about Steven. I received a short and not-so-sweet return email: *He's no longer with the company.*

Steven was a classic example of high Sales IQ and low Sales EQ. He was the smartest guy in the room that no one liked. He didn't have the ability to build trust and respect with his team or other managers at the company.

Emotion Management and Influence

Let's revisit the neuroscience of influence. An effective sales leader is good at emotion management and is consistent in how she shows up. This consistency builds sales cultures of trust because a key component of building trust is consistency. The sales team isn't worried about what type of emotional reaction will occur when they share a mistake with you. They don't have to watch and see what kind of mood you are in, before approaching with a question or problem.

Trust and respect are earned through congruency in what you say and do. Children observe the actions of their parents, not their words. Children grow up to be salespeople, ones with the same habits of observation. Salespeople watch a sales leader's actions more than their words.

They watch to see if you:

- Remain calm in the face of adversity
- Are respectful in conversations . . . even when you are upset

- Listen to all aspects of a situation before jumping to a hasty conclusion
- Are fully present in all conversations and meetings
- Demonstrate empathy or emotional apathy
- Are willing to hold the truth-telling, difficult conversations in an assertive, not aggressive manner

The Gift That Keeps on Giving—Mentorship

I was fortunate to have a great boss and mentor, Kline Boyd, when I was a vice president of sales. He possessed both Sales IQ and Sales EQ.

It was time to set sales budgets for the year. We were moving from an October to September fiscal calendar to a January through December fiscal calendar. It was a lot of numbers crunching and I asked my seven regional managers to turn in their sales projections for the year, providing them with the format with which to create their team's sales goals.

I don't recall exactly what I did wrong in the sales forecasting model, but it was wrong. My not-so-happy CFO informed me that I needed to start over and get the numbers to him ASAP as other departments were waiting on my sales numbers to complete budgets.

I was really upset and during my lunch break went to a nearby outdoor shopping complex and begin walking around. I dreaded the upcoming conversations with my regional sales managers. I was worried about how stupid I would sound when I had to tell Kline of my huge error. I was looking down, mumbling to myself, replaying worst-case scenarios in my head, and ran right into my boss. He noted my face and asked, "What's going on? Are you okay?" I did my best not to do the ugly cry.

"You didn't hear—I screwed up the entire sales forecast. We have to start all over."

I'll never forget his nonjudgmental, nonemotional reply. "Well, I guess you won't do that again." That was it. He knew I didn't need any lecture because he recognized I was doing an exceptional job of flogging myself. I have to admit that, at the time, I was too young to appreciate his calm, consistent demeanor and depth of emotional intelligence.

Today I do, and have shared his many words of wisdom long after working with him. Kline modeled the behavior he expected from others. He modeled great leadership, empathy, and emotion management, which earned him trust and respect from everyone who worked for him.

Look in the mirror. Are you modeling the emotional intelligence skills you expect from your sales team? I am a work in progress and certainly know that I've not liked the reflection I've seen in the mirror on more than one occasion.

The Sales Management Trigger-Response-Regret Loop

You've hired good salespeople and have invested time teaching them EQ skills needed to be successful in their role as sellers. But the fact is, you will still encounter situations where you need to hold a truth-telling conversation, a difficult conversation, even with very good salespeople. You hired a human being and human beings bring faults and blind spots that at certain times will need to be addressed. (If you are married, in a serious relationship, or raising children, you know what I'm talking about.)

For example, you're meeting with a salesperson who is behind plan for the first time in two years. You share the intent behind the coaching conversation, which is one of help and support. Your human salesperson starts lobbing excuses back to you. "You know, if I didn't have to spend all my time fielding questions because of our lousy delivery team, maybe I could sell something. I've checked out the competition . . . we are just too high-priced."

If you are like most of my high-achieving sales leaders, excuses are like nails on a chalkboard. Without self-awareness and emotion management, excuses can send you into the trigger-response-regret loop, elevating your "high need to be right" response. At this point, it's easy to turn into a trial lawyer, delivering a closing argument that that lays out solid answers to every excuse preventing success.

Your bad behavior flips on the salesperson's trigger-response-regret reaction. Now you are both fighting for the need to be right rather than the need to *get it right*. Little knowledge is transferred—and forget about any behavior changes. Emotions are running this conversation, not effective coaching and training skills.

Our logical, rational brain recognizes these reactions are not the correct responses. But when emotions start running conversations, the reptilian brain takes over, bringing with it the fight or flight reactions. Good coaching and rapport skills are nowhere to be found. It's the classic sales management knowing and doing gap.

Take Your Own Medicine

You've taught your team the power of downtime and reflection. Make sure you walk the walk and instill this powerful daily habit into your own morning routine. Your emails and texts can wait—you really aren't that important. Sorry.

If you didn't handle a conversation well with a salesperson, carve out quiet time and get to the root cause of your reaction.

That which you are not aware of you cannot change. That which you are not aware of you are bound to repeat.

The root cause for your emotional reaction might be the same as those discussed in chapter thirteen. Look in the mirror and examine your belief systems and the stories you are telling yourself about the salesperson. Stories create emotions, which affect the actions we take or don't take. Emotions affect the skills we apply or don't apply. A negative story about a salesperson creates negative emotions, which create trigger-response-regret coaching conversations.

Here are stories that I've heard from more than one sales manager when presenting this concept during our sales management workshops:

- He's just lazy and doesn't want to do the work.
- If she didn't have something to complain about, she wouldn't be happy.
- He is always looking for a magic formula for success.
- She doesn't care if the company loses money on this deal. That's why she keeps discounting.
- He is just trying to protect his territory and knowledge by not putting data into the CRM system.

Look at those stories. Are they going to create positive emotions and positive coaching conversations? Uh, no.

Get Curious

A coaching tool that I've learned from other leadership experts such as Keith Rosen, author of *Sales Leadership*, and Brene Brown, author of *Dare to Lead*, is to shift my negative self-talk from judgment to curiosity. Keith Rosen advises sales managers to get "radically curious." I've found that a curious mindset shifts my thinking from judgment and head know-it-all to that of an investigator. I become an observer of the conversation, rather than a fixer of the conversation. My investigator role keeps me curious and focused on examining any and all clues to solve the mystery of why a salesperson isn't executing the right selling behaviors.

Curiosity thinking forces you to ask yourself questions that create different answers:

- What else could be true? (Maybe the salesperson is embarrassed. Everyone else on the team is having a killer year.)
- Wonder what's really going on here? (Worry. The salesperson was planning on her quarterly bonus for her son's college fund.)
- What part of this story am I making up? (Are these excuses really self-doubt in disguise?)

Asking questions moves the conversation from your reptilian brain that is busy fueling your emotions and fears to the problem-solving part of your brain. This shift allows you to apply the hard skills, the coaching skills, needed to diagnose the sales performance issue. Curiosity thinking moves you from the need to *be right* to the need to *get it right*.

Take a lesson from Brian Grazer. He is the producer of such movies as *Apollo 13*, *A Beautiful Mind*, and *Splash*. He's also the author of *A Curious Mind: The Secret to a Bigger Life*. Brian has engaged in hundreds of "curiosity conversations" with people from all walks of life. Those conversations reward him with the gift of perspective, new insights, and different points of view. Grazer points out that you have to care about someone to wonder about them. When you sincerely wonder about a person, you naturally ask more questions and better questions.

Sales managers, if you really care about your salesperson, get really curious about the truth for lack of sales performance. Ask more questions, better questions, and you might just find the answers are totally different than the story you are making up about the salesperson.

Curiosity Sales Coaching

Take a look at some common sales coaching scenarios where sales managers fall into defensive coaching behaviors rather than curiosity coaching behaviors.

Scenario One

Salesperson: "You know, I just have a bad territory."

Defensive sales management response: "Your territory actually has more qualified prospects than other regions across the country. In fact, let me show you the data."

Curiosity questions: "Is it a bad territory or do you have a really tough competitor in this territory? Is it a bad territory or do you need more help in strategizing on how to connect with the right prospects in the territory?"

Scenario Two

Salesperson: "Our marketing collateral is outdated."

Defensive sales management response: "The marketing department just updated this collateral. Compared to the competition, it's twice as good. When I started in sales, we didn't even have a marketing department and I still hit quota." (And I walked ten miles to school . . .)

Curiosity questions: "Tell me more about what is outdated. What are you hoping marketing collateral could do to help you win more business? What does updated look like?"

Scenario Three

Salesperson: "I could win more business if we just had better pricing."

Defensive sales management response: "We have plenty of customers that are buying our products and services at full price. Let's talk one more time about selling value, not price."

Curiosity questions: "Is it our pricing or are you targeting the wrong clients? When you have won business at full margin, what have you found to be the common theme for winning this type of business [i.e., pain point, competitor, trigger event]?"

Apply the same soft skills you are teaching your sales team. Examine your self-limiting beliefs, your stories. Become a sales investigator and apply curiosity. The shift will help you execute the hard skills, the coaching skills, of sales management.

Empathy and Influence

As discussed in chapter twelve, empathy is the mega influence skill. And boy, can we blow it in sales leadership. I certainly have.

It's easy to fall into the "my intent is good but my approach was way off" program. In a desire to help your sales team improve, sales managers forget the power of empathy and influence. Sales leaders are assertive and good problem solvers. However, those same skills can become their Achilles' heel. When a salesperson presents a problem, the sales manager puts on her fix-it hat and immediately starts offering advice.

The problem is, salespeople can't hear your great advice until you've demonstrated that you've heard them. They are just like your prospects and customers. They are human beings who have an inherent desire to be understood.

In your fast-paced world as a sales manager, apply self-awareness. You are busy and may want to "rush empathy." Sorry, empathy can't be rushed. Empathy is a paying attention skill. You must be present to win. It requires being highly aware of how you show up to daily conversations and coaching sessions. Make a decision where you want to be. Focus and pay attention.

Be here now.

Grow Your Sales Management Empathy Skills

Empathy is developed by tuning into your own emotions, what you are thinking or feeling. How can sales managers possibly influence salespeople, human beings, if they don't know what their sales team is thinking or feeling?

They can't.

In the quiet, reflect on various selling scenarios you experienced as a seller. Did you ever:

- Feel intimidated by a prospect or customer? What thoughts went through your head?
- Experience self-doubt? What were you thinking or feeling?
- Feel discouraged because nothing seemed to be working or closing?

Dig beneath the superficial layers of thinking, which lead to generic labeling of emotions and canned coaching conversations.

Take time to reflect and tune into your emotions, which in turn helps you tune into the emotional state of your salespeople.

See Figure 18.1 for the "S" framework we teach to move beyond superficial and generic coaching conversations.

THE "S" FRAMEWORK OF EMPATHY

Slow down.

Stop to think.

Step into your salesperson's shoes.

State what the salesperson is thinking or feeling.

Be **Still** and listen to their **Story**.

FIGURE 18.1

For example, a salesperson states emphatically that the new CRM system is too difficult. Now, you know from other members of your sales team that the new CRM system is easier and twice as effective as the old system. Your initial response might be to make up a story about the salesperson. "This salesperson is always pushing back on change." Or, you get emotionally triggered and start defending and justifying the new system. To build your case, you share success stories from salespeople on the team who aren't having any problems with the new CRM system.

Yeah, this is a great way to make an emotional connection and build trust.

Slow down. *Stop* and really think about your salesperson's perspective, whether you agree with it or not. (Easier said than done.)

Step into your salesperson's shoes. Empathy is being able to hear the conversation that is not being said. What the salesperson is *not* saying is that change is difficult. This conversation is not about the new CRM system. This conversation is about change. The salesperson is still in the hard phase of learning. She's not a digital native, so technology is intimidating to her. The change to the new CRM means it takes more time for her to complete tasks.

The empathetic sales manager *states* what the salesperson is *not* saying, what she's really thinking or feeling: "I am guessing that your frustration with the new CRM system is because it's slowing you down, which is taking time away from revenue-generating activities. And it certainly doesn't help when you see other salespeople liking the new system when it's only bogging you down. Am I reading this situation correctly?"

When you hear a resounding yes, you've achieved empathy. Be *still* and avoid moving into solving the problem. Ask questions to learn the salesperson's *story*. "Tell me more what's going on." Effective coaching is just like good selling skills. You need to hear the salesperson's story before you can offer solutions.

Once you learn more of your salesperson's story, then and only then can you move to a coaching and training conversation. Salespeople can't hear your great advice until like they feel you've heard them and understood them.

Empathy and Effective Sales Coaching

John is a great sales leader, and after completing several of our courses, he shared with me new insights gained from increased self-awareness. "I had no idea that I was putting members of my sales team into a fight or flight emotional state. I've always invested time in debriefing sales calls, but now I realize that my debriefing sessions sounded like an interrogation, rather than a helpful coaching session. It's no wonder my sales team often defaulted to defending and justifying their actions. I didn't demonstrate empathy when a salesperson would bring me a loss and ask for coaching. My immediate response was to focus on solving the problem to prevent it from happening again."

Salespeople can't hear your great advice until you've demonstrated you've heard them.

Sales Management Empathy Misses

Here are some other common examples of empathy misses in sales management. My observation in working with sales managers is their problem-solving approach is filled with good intent. They really want to help. But the coaching framework is incorrect. Sales managers: empathy first, advice second.

Take a look at some coaching scenarios where well-intentioned sales managers reverse the framework, offering advice first.

Sales Scenario

A salesperson has been working on a deal for nine months. A new decision maker has joined the company and is bringing in a past relationship to now be considered for the work.

Possible response by sales manager: "Well, let's strategize on how we can gain access to this new buyer. We can still win this business. What questions should we ask to best position ourselves?"

Empathetic response: "That's a bummer. You've worked so hard on this deal and now it looks like you have to start all over. And on top of that, you're probably feeling a little betrayed that your internal champions aren't doing more to move the deal your way. Am I correct or off base?"

Sales Scenario

A salesperson has been doing all the right activities and is still not filling the sales pipeline.

Possible response by sales manager: "Okay, let's look at the activity plan again and specific tactics associated with those. We can turn this around."

Empathetic response: "You've got to be feeling a little discouraged because you are doing all the right things and yet nothing is popping. And you might even be wondering if you have what it takes to make it in this position. Am I correct?"

Sales Scenario

A salesperson has a longtime customer who is really upset with him because of missed deadlines caused by another department in the company.

Possible response by sales manager: "I'm happy to get on the phone and deal with the customer. I'm so tired of department XYZ falling short."

Empathetic response: "Those are really tough calls to take and I know you must be feeling a little unappreciated because the customer doesn't seem to remember all the extras you've done for their company. And it certainly doesn't help when you didn't create the problem. Am I correct?"

Salespeople can't hear your great coaching advice until they feel like you've heard them.

Emotional Self-Awareness, Assertiveness, and Crucial Sales Conversations

There is a great book titled *Crucial Conversations* authored by Patterson, Grenny, McMillan, and Switzler. The focus of the book is teaching managers and leaders how to effectively hold the difficult conversations, the crucial conversations.

I also call these conversations truth-telling conversations. They aren't easy conversations and many of us are average, at best, in holding them. Remember, you can hire a great salesperson but chances are at some point you will need to hold a truth-telling conversation.

Organizations grow and change in order to remain relevant. This means your sales team will need to grow and change. People don't like change because it represents the unknown.

The unknown represents the possibility to fail so human beings resist new ideas and ways of conducting business, even when the new ways of conducting business will ensure future success.

Emotion management, assertiveness, and self-awareness are key emotional intelligence skills in holding truth-telling conversations.

What Makes Truth-Telling Conversations Difficult?

No one looks forward to a difficult conversation. Can't we all just get along? When I dig into the real reason sales leaders aren't holding truth-telling sales conversations, I find the emotion of fear rearing its ugly head again.

Fear is one of the big reasons people in general aren't assertive in stating what they need. They fear losing something, and as a result, aren't assertive in nicely asking for what they need.

- Parents don't discipline their children for fear of losing their love.
- Spouses put up with rude and condescending behavior for fear their spouse will leave.
- Customers don't send cold food back in restaurants for fear of the waitstaff not liking them. (Or something worse.)

Sales managers are not assertive in asking for what they need and, in many cases, put up with inappropriate selling behaviors because of fear.

- Fear the salesperson will leave and take the company's best clients.
- Fear the salesperson will leave and be hard to replace. Your industry isn't that sexy and it's hard to find good salespeople.
- Fear the sales team won't like you. Your need for approval is getting in the way of asking for what you and the company need.
- Fear that a truth-telling conversation will change the sales culture.

Hello. Time for a Reality Check

During our Ei Sales Management Training Program, I conduct an exercise asking participants to write down the name of an acquaintance and the name of a really close friend or relative. Then, I ask them to write down if they've ever had a conflict with the acquaintance, close friend, or relative.

About 95 percent of the time, participants write that they have not had a conflict with an acquaintance. But almost 100 percent will state they've had a conflict with a close friend or relative. This exercise raises self-awareness around the topic of conflict. The reality is, the closer the relationship you have with a person, the greater the probability you will need to engage in a truth-telling conversation.

Denial and Caretaking Sales Cultures

Several years ago, I met with a very nice CEO who proudly shared the history of her company and their family culture, their nurturing culture. But the more we talked, the more I realized she didn't have a nurturing culture; she had a caretaking culture. This "family" was a cross between an adult nursery and a senior retirement home. Reps were whining about everything (nursery) and many had settled into complacency (retirement home).

This very nice CEO was in denial. What she described as a nurturing culture was really a sales culture that avoided accountability and difficult conversations. Her inability to hold the difficult conversations was the root cause for declining revenues and a culture of entitlement. When I asked questions around accountability and responsibility, she gave several excuses as to why she couldn't set expectations for new selling behaviors needed to remain relevant in a changing business environment. However, their competition wasn't whining or retired on the job. They were busy taking this company's best customers!

This CEO lacked the assertiveness to hold truth-telling conversations with her team. We agreed not to do business because success would require changes she was not willing to make.

Assertive, Aggressive, or Passive Coaching Behaviors

Many sales managers possess high assertiveness because this is a soft skill found in many top sales producers. But the demonstration of this soft skill can be situational—and I have observed more than one sales manager not bringing this important skill into their sales leadership role. It often disappears when conducting the crucial sales coaching sessions. Sales leaders default to aggressive coaching behaviors or passive-aggressive coaching behaviors.

If a sales manager hasn't fully mastered self-control and emotion management, the likely default is an aggressive approach. The sales manager tells the salesperson, in no uncertain terms, what changes are expected. The delivery of the message is accompanied by tense tonality matched by an even more tense facial expression. This approach kicks off the trigger-response-regret loop between the sales manager and the salesperson. A salesperson might respond defensively, which escalates the conversation. Or, she might respond in a passive-aggressive manner, appearing to agree with expectations laid out by the sales manager. But silently, the salesperson is resentful and has no intention of doing anything the sales manager has suggested. The result is little change in selling behaviors. And the sales manager is revisiting the exact same issues the following month.

Without self-awareness, sales managers can default to passive-aggressive coaching behaviors during the crucial coaching conversations. Fear makes another guest appearance. The first sign of pushback from the salesperson on expected changes leads to "okey dokey" behavior from the sales manager. "I can't lose this salesperson. I don't have anyone to put in this position. He might go to the competition and take all of our customers."

The sales manager goes along to get along and doesn't stay firm on the new expectations needed for success. "Well, let's talk about this again." (Like in the next fifty years.) The sales manager and salesperson hold the same conversation over and over again because the passive-aggressive sales manager isn't assertive enough to finish the difficult coaching conversation.

Assertive sales managers are comfortable holding truth-telling conversations around improvements in selling behaviors such as poor attitude, missed sales results, lack of following necessary processes, or being a better team player.

The assertive sales manager brings a combination of EQ skills to the difficult coaching conversations—skills such as self-awareness, empathy, and assertiveness. She is aware of triggers that cause her to default to aggressive or passive coaching behaviors. She brings empathy to establish the foundation for a good conversation. And she brings assertiveness to state expectations and changes needed in a manner that can be heard and received.

Let's take a look at what a self-aware, empathetic, assertive truth-telling coaching conversation might sound like regarding a veteran salesperson's lack of participation in the monthly group sales meeting.

"Jim, I wanted to address your lack of participation in the group sales meetings. First of all, I do want you to know how much I appreciate your consistency in achieving goals . . . I never worry about you or your work ethic. And if I were in your shoes, I'd actually be wondering one of two things [Empathy]:

- Why do I have to attend these meetings? I'm hitting quota.
- These meetings just take me away from making more sales."

"Am I correct?"

"Yes. No offense, but I find sales meetings a waste of time. I think you should just spend time with the salespeople who need help instead of making the rest of us sit in meetings, listening to their problems." (Watch your emotional response to Jim's answer.)

"Well, that makes perfect sense." (Apply empathy and assertiveness. Stay the course.) "Here's the problem. Maybe you can help and maybe you can't. We are growing and adding a lot of new salespeople. Like me, you were here in the early days. And if you remember, one of the reasons we've experienced success is that, in the early days, we all had each other's back. We did a lot of sharing and brainstorming, which helped everyone close business. Would you agree or am I making this story up?"

"Yeah . . . I remember. Those early days were tough. We didn't have a brand or market share."

"Well, I know this type of collaboration is the winning formula for future success and I need your help. As the top producer, I need you to show up to meetings, put aside your other work, and be open to sharing your expertise and experience, which will help ramp up our new hires to quicker success. Our sales team is only as good as its weakest link, and I want to make sure all of our links are strong. It's two hours out of your month . . . can you do that?"

"Yes . . . two hours isn't going to kill me. Got it."

The emotionally intelligent sales manager works hard at developing emotion management, empathy, and assertiveness skills. This powerful combination of EQ skills allows you to effectively hold truth-telling conversations.

Mirror, mirror, on the wall, are you modeling what you are teaching at all?

Sales Leaders EQ Action Steps

1. Carve out quiet time and examine the negative stories you might be making up about members of your sales team.
2. Develop your curiosity skills. Put on your sales investigator hat during coaching conversations.
3. Bring the powerful skill of empathy to your coaching conversations.
4. Practice the "S" framework of empathy.
5. Review and analyze recent coaching conversations. Did you demonstrate assertiveness, passive-aggressive, or aggressive communication skills?

The Neuroscience of Teaching and Coaching

MANY YEARS AGO, I heard Pam Gordon speak. She is an award-winning former principal and expert on adult learning. She shared great insights around the adult learning model to help speakers and trainers avoid the curse of, "That was a great presentation. Too bad none of the participants will remember or apply anything you said." Information and knowledge are power, but only when applied.

As I listened to Pam, I experienced another one of my "duh" moments. "Duh, this is why sales managers have trouble transferring the knowledge that made them so successful. This is why really good salespeople often don't make the leap to sales leadership." Successful salespeople often fail in their new role as sales manager because they've never learned the fundamentals of teaching, which is an essential skill for developing salespeople.

As the late, legendary basketball coach John Wooden said, "Don't equate your expertise with your ability to teach."

Think about it. Professional teachers attend four years of college in order to learn how to teach their future students. Professional coaches attend specific courses to earn their coaching certificates. Where do sales manager earn their teaching degrees? The University of Hard Knocks and Headaches.

Effective sales managers know how to transfer the knowledge, habits, and skills that made them a top producer. A sales manager's goal is to *not* be the smartest guy or gal in the room. If you are, then you can look forward to being the full-time chief problem solver and/or closer at your company.

The Neuroscience of Sales Mastery

I addressed the concept of neuroplasticity in my first book and it's important to revisit. Without this knowledge, sales managers become frustrated, wondering why their sales team isn't executing the knowledge and skills they are teaching.

For many years, the belief in the scientific world was that the brain was fixed, having a specific number of neurons performing functions in a set way. Research now shows that the brain is capable of learning new ways of doing and being because it can form new neural pathways. The process is called neuroplasticity. Hebb's law describes this process as, "Cells that fire together, wire together."

Repetition is the key to forming these new neural pathways, which allow new ways of thinking and doing. However, practicing a selling skill one time will not create a new set of connections in your salesperson's brain. Study masterful people in any profession and you will find the common denominator is the amount of time devoted to practice.

Mastery of selling skills and emotional intelligence skills should be simple, right? Practice and repetition are totally within a salesperson's control. So why are so many salespeople and sales organizations stuck in their old ways of doing things?

Be Aware of the J Curve

If you've been in sales management long enough, you've observed the J curve. You teach your sales team a new selling skill, one that will positively change the outcome of sales meetings and sales results. This new skill is a very different approach than the one the salesperson has used for the last five years.

However, your salesperson is open to learning and is enthusiastic about applying her new skills at the next meeting with a prospect. As she applies her new skills, she stumbles in the execution—words coming out of her mouth are jumbled. She feels awkward using this new approach. Your open-to-learning salesperson is not so open anymore. She flees back to the comfort of what she knows, even if that approach produces less-than-average sales results.

I've heard and seen pushback on adoption of new skills more than once in my career as a sales leader and sales teacher.

"This won't work in our industry." (Note: The salesperson has never tried the new selling approach but is convinced the new approach won't work.)

"My old way is working . . . why do I need to try this approach?" (Maybe because you are writing more practice proposals than signed agreements.)

Welcome to the J curve. This theory was developed over one hundred years ago as a way of describing the economic behavior of nations. The premise is that, during periods of major change, things tend to get worse before they get better. This model has been used to describe the process of change, ranging from economics all the way to the learning performance of students.

Many sales managers don't know how to help their sales team navigate through times of change. They haven't learned how to lower their sales team's resistance to new ideas to avoid settling and status quo selling behaviors. As a result, they end up pushing, cajoling, and convincing with little or no change.

Take a look at the model below. The beginning of the letter is where your sales team's current selling and mindset skill sets are. They aren't bad, but they aren't good enough to win in an increasingly competitive business environment. When you teach your sales team new selling skills, there's a very good chance they will get worse before they get better because they haven't logged enough hours of practice to form new neural pathways. In the early stages of learning, their neural pathways look more like jumbled-up balls of string than the desired T-1 line of mastery (see Figure 19.1).

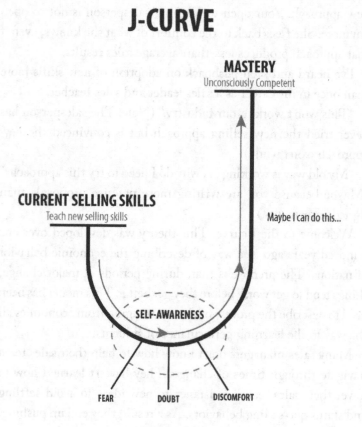

FIGURE 19.1

They start moving toward the bottom of the J curve. Here's where it's important to tune into your salesperson's emotional state. Take into account the salesperson's reptilian brain. This new approach is different and unknown, possible danger. At the bottom of the J curve, the learning curve, the reptilian brain kicks in and says:

- Danger . . . you don't know how to do this. You could fail.
- Play it safe. Your old approach to selling isn't that bad.
- Danger . . . you haven't mastered this skill. Don't do it—you'll look stupid in front of prospects and clients.
- Danger . . . this new approach looks like it is going to take a lot of time to learn and you are already swamped with work.

Sales leaders have to be aware of their own negative self-talk and poor impulse control at the bottom of the J curve. "It would be easier to close this deal myself. I don't have time to get this salesperson up to speed. This salesperson doesn't want to get better."

Don't give up. Keep reinforcing new skills, habits, and behaviors. Your hard work will pay off as you see the salesperson's skills improve and move up the other side of the J curve. You'll hear their self-talk change from, "I'm never going to get this," to "Hey, I'm getting good at this. Why didn't I learn this approach sooner?"

Mastery doesn't happen with one, two, or three repetitions. Depending on the complexity of the skill to be learned, new habits must be practiced and repeated daily. Research from the *European Journal of Social Psychology* shows that habit formation can take anywhere from 18 days to 254 days. Then and only then has the new information landed in the long-term memory area of the brain, the basal ganglia.

Learning and mastering new skills and habits is hard work. Dr. Tara Swart, a senior lecturer at MIT and author of the book *Neuroscience for Leadership*, shares that the "brain is inherently lazy and will usually choose the most energy efficient path if we let it."

The brain is the most energy-demanding organ, using half of all the sugar energy in the body. When a person is learning something new, the brain becomes an energy-sucking machine. No wonder salespeople quit at the bottom of the J curve and continue to use old, outdated approaches to sales. It's much easier to be average than excellent.

Sales managers, apply your delayed gratification skills and avoid the pull of instant gratification and "one and done" sales training. You know what I'm talking about. You invest in one sales training course and now your sales team is trained—for the rest of their lives!

Revisit your coaching and training calendars. What selling skills have you practiced with your sales team on a daily or weekly basis? Have you reinforced desired selling behaviors with your team for 18 days? 254 days? If you aren't reinforcing new concepts long enough or frequently enough, your sales team will wallow at the bottom of the J curve and be highly tempted to run back to comfort zones and "good enough" selling skills.

Teach your sales team the concepts around learning and the J curve. This knowledge normalizes the natural challenges that accompany mastery. Instead of feeling like losers, your sales team will learn that struggle and discomfort are a normal part of up-leveling skills and knowledge.

Normalize Failure

One of my favorite stories around mastery and the J curve comes from one of our clients, Charles Avila. He had just graduated from Stanford University with an engineering degree and was hired by a firm selling test equipment for engineers. While he definitely had the Sales IQ down, he also had high self-awareness and self-esteem to recognize he didn't know anything about sales. He enrolled in one of our sales training and coaching programs and was a great student. One day he called into our office, and reached out to Gail, one of our sales consultants. Gail thought Charles was calling to report the good news of landing a big account or exceeding his sales goal. But Charles was excited about something else. "Gail, I'm at the bottom of the J curve!" He was excited because he knew the only direction in his level of selling skills was up. He wasn't experiencing self-doubt or worry because we'd normalized the process of failing while doing the hard work of learning new skills. He understood that sometimes you get worse before you get better.

Sales Physiology

When people are learning new skills, the brain's hippocampus—a seahorse-shaped structure that plays critical roles in processing, storing, and recalling information—is necessary for declarative memory. Salespeople can try multitasking and learning but the retention and recall factor goes down. New information doesn't get cemented into long-term memory. As a result, the salesperson and company waste time and money because they can't recall or apply the new learnings.

Russell Poldrack, UCLA associate professor of psychology, coauthored a study with the National Academy of Sciences on how multitasking affects learning and retention. "Even if you learn while multi-tasking, that learning is less flexible and more specialized, so you cannot retrieve the information as easily."

It's the paper, rock, and scissors game again. This time the rock is multitasking and the scissors are learning. If your sales team is multitasking during training or coaching sessions, the rock of multitasking will always smash learning. A salesperson won't be able to recall the needed information on that next critical sales call and will conduct an average sales meeting. If you're going to allow multitasking during sales training and coaching sessions, don't bother investing the time or money. You'll get a higher return on investment taking your sales team to dinner. It's up to you to model the discipline required to achieve sales mastery.

The Myth of Age and Attention Spans

We work with PopSockets, based out of Boulder, Colorado. It's a true global success story. The founder, David Barnett, started the company working out of his garage. Many of you reading this book have this innovative product on the back of your smartphones. I have to admit I was a little skeptical about how this group of millennials, working in the tech space, would respond to our no-tech rule. To my surprise—and delight—this sales team was terrific. They didn't engage in the stealth, looking-at-the-phone-under-the-table behavior. (What is that about?) They paid attention even though their phones and computers were blowing up with customer requests, orders, and questions. When I sat down to review the engagement with Bob Africa, their chief of staff, I kiddingly asked if he had threatened the team if they got distracted with technology during the training. He laughed and said, "No, I told you when we first met. This young sales team is really eager to learn. I simply asked them to give full attention to the training and they did."

So much for the arguments around age, paying attention, and multitasking.

Keep in mind that the mega tech companies of the world aren't helping sales managers. They have neuroscientists on their teams who know how to manipulate the brain and program technology to feed the cycle of addiction. They understand that when a person checks a text or email, it releases a bump of the feel-good hormone dopamine, which activates the reward center of the brain.

Learning and developing new neural pathways is hard work. The J curve is uncomfortable. Practice can be tedious because, in the learning phase, there's no reward. It's no wonder sales managers and salespeople default to checking email and texts. Those behaviors are rewarded with a nice dopamine bump!

My personal philosophy is that I refuse to be a lab rat for these companies. Our sales and management training workshops are technology-free zones. We know the power of being fully present in order to learn new information. We are highly focused and passionate about salespeople learning concepts and skills that will position them as a trusted advisor rather than a run-of-the-mill transactional salesperson.

Do the hard work of learning.

The Sales Checklist Manifesto

I've always been a fan of studying other professions to gain new insights on how to improve sales and sales management skills. One such profession is that of medicine and the work of Atul Gawande, author of *The Checklist Manifesto: How to Get Things Right.*

"Our great struggle in medicine these days is not just with ignorance and uncertainty," Gawande says. "It's also with complexity: How much you have to make sure you have in your head and think about. There are a thousand ways things can go wrong."

Gawande introduced his two-minute checklist into operating rooms in eight hospitals and immediately saw better results by catching basic mistakes. Doctors and nurses are human, and as a result, can miss things or make mistakes. Surgery and medicine are complex, with a lot of moving parts and a lot of information to keep track of.

The practice of medicine sounds like the practice of sales. Salespeople are human and can miss things or make mistakes. Sales is complex, with a lot of moving parts and information. A checklist helps all salespeople be more effective in sales, regardless of the number of years in the business.

Checklists also help combat the Dunning-Kruger Effect. Coined in 1999 by then-Cornell psychologists David Dunning and Justin Kruger, this is a cognitive bias whereby people who are incompetent at something are unable to recognize their own incompetence. In very simple terms, we are all guilty of thinking we are doing something better than we actually are. (I still think I should be onstage singing somewhere.)

More than one sales manager has worked with a salesperson who truly believes he is running an effective sales call. Telling the salesperson how and where to improve is going to fall on deaf ears because of the salesperson's false belief around his ability. Apply principles from the adult learning model. People believe their own data, and a checklist is a great way of providing objective data by which the salesperson can check if he is running an effective sales meeting or not. A checklist helps a salesperson determine if she asked all the questions to complete a selling stage.

A common area where I've consistently seen salespeople suffer from the Dunning-Kruger Effect is in diagnosing a prospect's problem or real goal. Many salespeople hear the presenting problem but don't ask further questions to learn the implications behind the presenting problem.

For example, a prospect shares the presenting problem of, "We need better quality." With a strong sales checklist, a salesperson is able to see if she uncovered the true implication of poor quality or settled for a superficial sales conversation. A checklist could include:

- **Financial implication questions**
  How much is poor quality costing this prospect?

And because of this cost, what other areas of the company
are being affected?
Is dealing with poor quality and redos causing budget
overruns? How much?
- **Strategic implication questions**
How is poor quality affecting the prospect's reputation?
Is poor quality affecting the company's ability to scale?
How is this problem affecting your initiative to move into
new markets?
- **Personal implication questions**
How much time is the prospect spending on issues related
to poor quality?
What's not getting done because of the time that is being
spent on fixing quality problems?
What kind of pressure is the prospect feeling from his
boss or customers?

Checklists take away the cognitive bias of "I did a great job on
this sales call." Checklists force objective measures, which in turn
forces the salesperson to examine if she actually did say and do
what she was supposed to during a sales call.

We've created a variety of checklists for clients that range from
prospecting activities to detailed questions that should be asked
during each qualifying stage of the sales process.

Take a look at your sales team's recent sales conversations and
outcomes. How many could have been improved by incorporating
the power of sales checklists?

Stories and Skill Building

Study great teachers and influencers, and you will find that they've
mastered the power of stories. We've all heard a great speaker at

some point in our careers. And I bet you remember the stories told, rather than the facts and figures shared.

The brain is wired for stories and effective sales leaders use this tool to teach, inspire, and motivate their sales teams. Stories activate chemicals in the brain that improve awareness and help people feel good, inspiring them to take action.

Great teachers have the ability to make information stick and use stories to teach and motivate. It's easy for sales leaders to miss the power of storytelling and default to PowerPoint presentations or sharing of facts and figures. The concepts presented are great. The delivery . . . not so much. The sales team checks out and the sales manager is stuck teaching the same concepts over and over.

Incorporate storytelling into your daily training and coaching processes. With every sales skill you teach, I challenge you to accompany the teaching of each selling skill with a story.

Sales Coaching through Stories

One of my clients uses a great story to demonstrate the formal and informal process behind a company's decision-making process. It would have been easy for this sales manager to be the sage on the stage and teach his sales team terms such as economic buyer, user buyer, technical buyer, and influencer buyer. Blah, blah, blah. Instead, he shared a personal story to illustrate the importance of identifying all the buying influences.

"I started my sales career with a small company that was doubling revenues year over year. Our IT systems were bursting at the seams and it was time to install a new ERP system. We paraded very smart consultants through the office and they met with all the obvious decision makers: the CIO, the CFO, and the CEO. If you had a C in your title, you got a meeting!

"All the consulting firms did a good job of writing comprehensive recommendations. They were likeable and polished at presenting their recommendations. But we ended up choosing the most expensive consulting firm because this was the only firm that uncovered the HDM: hidden decision maker. Her name was Terri and she was the customer service manager. She'd been with the company since the beginning. Terri managed the order entry department, worked closely with the warehouse, and knew everything about everything. Terri was loved by her team so if Terri thought something needed to be done, that was good enough for her team.

"Even though Terri had a C in her title, it wasn't a big enough C to warrant a meeting with most of the consulting firms, except one. The consulting firm that won the project uncovered the HDM by asking one question: 'Who's the person at the company that I should know, but I don't know?' The consistent answer was, 'Oh, you need to meet Terri.' The winning firm conducted that interview, and as a result, gathered additional intel that was important to the success of the new system."

That's a great story and a great teaching tool. This story demonstrates the importance of uncovering all the decision makers *and* the true decision maker. It creates positive stress for the sales team, making them wonder who is the hidden decision maker in their current sales pipeline. The brain likes stories. Help your sales team learn and apply more information by incorporating storytelling into coaching and training sessions.

Great sales leaders know how to transfer the knowledge, habits, and skills that made them a top producer. Learn and master the skills of teaching and coaching. Learn how to be a more effective sales leader.

Sales Leaders EQ Action Plan

1. Learn and study the principles of adult learning. Understand how to transfer the knowledge that made you successful.
2. Teach your team the J curve. Normalize the difficulty of sales mastery.
3. Stop multitasking to ensure that knowledge can be learned and retrieved. Make a decision where you want to be.
4. Create a checklist sales manifesto for your various selling stages and skills.
5. Incorporate storytelling into your sales training and coaching.

20

Sales
Is Not
a Department

MEET YOUR ENTIRE SALES team. Pete is the office manager and is the first person most prospects and clients interface with on the phone or in person. Joan is the head of customer service. Her team troubleshoots client problems and questions. Frank is the warehouse manager and oversees all shipping and receivables. Cynthia is the chief marketing officer and is charged with all things marketing, including lead generation for your sales team. Danita is the director of IT and oversees the technical staff that installs your product and services.

Sales is not a department. Each person at your company has the ability to make a first impression, second impression, and third impression on your prospects and clients. That impression and interaction may very well determine whether this client becomes an advocate for your company or your competitor's next client.

Unfortunately, many members of your extended sales team haven't been taught formal sales, communication, or emotional intelligence skills. This thinking is really shortsighted because these individuals are the very people handling the sale after the sale. These teams install your product and services. They troubleshoot issues and questions with customers. They educate customers on how to use a new product or service, ensuring the customer feels that they are receiving a return on investment.

Think about how client conversations would be enhanced if everyone at your company received education around:

- Communicating with different personality styles
- Empathy
- Emotion management
- Emotional self-awareness
- Impulse control
- Assertiveness

Without proper training and education, the client experience is diminished. Those hard-earned new clients that come in the front door too often take a quick exit out the back door. Research shows that U.S. companies lose $136 billion to avoidable consumer switching. Ouch!

According to research by the Peppers & Rogers Group, customers rely on their emotional experiences with salespeople more than any of the traditional factors. They found that 60 percent of all customers stop dealing with a company because of what they perceive as indifference on the part of salespeople.

This interpretation of indifference often occurs because the sale-after-the-sale team is not provided with emotional intelligence skill training, particularly training in empathy. Sales is not a department, and every interaction with a customer is a chance to enhance the sale or blow the sale.

**Your support team and anyone interfacing
with customers is a salesperson;
they are part of the sales team!**

Empathy and the Sale after the Sale

Reflect on your own experiences in buying a product or service. Perhaps you've experienced something similar to the scenario below.

Cynthia has set aside two precious hours of time to wait for the cable tech. She waits and waits and waits and finally receives a call from Joe, the customer service person. The conversation sounds like, "Cynthia, I understand the tech missed the two-hour window. I know this is frustrating. Thank you for your business."

Cynthia becomes even more upset, thinking, "If you understood my frustration, you'd do a better job of describing it!" The trigger-response-regret loop starts and Cynthia vents mightily at Joe, who is helplessly staring at his new certificate that reads Customer Relationship Graduate.

This entire conversation would change if the person dealing with an upset client had been taught real-world empathy. Joe could have diffused Cynthia's anger by demonstrating that he really did understand what she was thinking or feeling around a missed appointment. Let me give you an example of *extreme* empathy using the same example.

Joe calls Cynthia and demonstrates real-world empathy, *extreme* empathy. "Cynthia, I understand our tech, Pete, missed the two-hour window." Pause. "You must think he's a moron. And I am sure you're really ticked off because you have a busy schedule and we managed to waste two hours of that schedule. Now, you're wondering how in the heck you are going to be able to fit a new appointment in your calendar. Oh, and on top of that, you had a lot of companies from which to choose to do business and you are wondering why did I choose XYZ company? Am I correct?"

Yes, that's an example of *extreme* empathy. And it's exactly what the customer is thinking. This type of conversation actually diffuses the emotional reaction from customers because they feel heard and understood. Customers recognize they don't have to fight for their position anymore. Their fear of not being understood fades away.

Am I advocating that you throw your fellow team members or company under the bus? Of course not. The example is to get your attention and get you focused on teaching the sale-after-the-sale team empathy skills.

Customers can't hear solutions to fixing a problem until they know and believe your entire sales team understands their perspective. In today's competitive business environment, customers that don't feel an emotional connection take their business elsewhere.

Empathy Changes the Conversation

We worked with a large distribution company's sales support team a few years ago. If you know anything about distribution, it's an industry that will experience fulfillment issues, even at well-run companies. Missed deadlines, wrong product ordered, wrong product shipped, incorrect color, and the list goes on. During our assessment, we discovered the root cause for many of the fulfillment issues were actually mistakes made by the customer. The sales manager and sales team recognized it didn't matter who caused the problem. They focused on getting it right rather than being right. Their goal was to provide extreme customer support. We conducted real-world empathy sales training and the team got it. They did a terrific job of changing the conversation when receiving calls from upset customers. Here are a few examples of the responses we co-created with the team in dealing with customer service issues:

- "Sorry for the stress we are causing you because I'm guessing your customers are upset, calling you nonstop because of this missed deadline."

- "I'm so sorry you're having to deal with this because I'm pretty sure you have fifteen other priorities that have to get done. And now, you have to waste time calling me to fix a problem that shouldn't have happened in the first place."

The team reported great success in diffusing frustrated clients. They found that customers were open to hearing new ways of preventing problems because the customers felt like the support team understood their world. The empathy first and advice second principle worked well in creating an emotional connection with customers and preventing future problems.

Get Out of Your Office and into Your Customer's Office

How many people in your company, other than salespeople, meet with clients on a regular basis to truly understand a day in the life of your customers? There is nothing that replaces time spent with clients and hearing firsthand what's working or not working.

I was reminded of this important practice while reading Melinda Gates's book, *The Moment of Lift*. The Gates Foundation is doing remarkable work around the world. One of the many reasons for their success is that members of their team aren't making decisions just from Excel spreadsheets and data. They are doing the hard work of traveling to remote villages and connecting face-to-face with the very people they are trying to help. What they've learned over the years is that you can't come up with the right solutions if you aren't talking to the people on the inside, in their case, impoverished women and children.

Take a lesson from the Gates Foundation and get members of your team into your customers' villages. Talk to the people on the inside, your customers. During those conversations, your team will hear firsthand the new demands your customers are facing from their customers. They'll hear new threats your customers are facing from new competitors or industry disruption. The only way your company can create new and better solutions is to get out of the office and into the offices of clients. Your customers are the insiders that have the answers.

It might behoove the director of operations to accompany salespeople on account business review calls. These conversations allow her to hear what your company and their department can do to make life easier for customers.

Schedule calls with your top clients and your customer service director. Surveys are nice, but live conversations are even better. Follow Janelle Barlow's advice. She is a customer service expert and teaches her clients to proactively seek out complaints. Barlow knows that complaints are a gift because research shows that most customers don't complain. They just go away.

Check out these stats: 96 percent of unhappy customers don't complain; however, 91 percent of those unhappy customers will simply leave and never come back, according to 1 Financial Training Services.

Why don't customers complain? Many feel it's too much work. Others feel that it just won't make any difference. That attitude changes dramatically when you've got a live human being sitting in front of you sincerely asking for your complaints and insights on how to better partner with you.

Relationships Start at Home

No one has time for relationships. You make time for relationships. Why do you think couples schedule date night?

Relationships start at home and they start with you, Mr. or Ms. Sales Leader, building relationships with your extended sales team and the other departments that help your sales team retain and serve clients. It takes a sales village to win and retain business. Schedule time to visit other departments to observe a day in their lives.

It Takes a Sales Village

One of our sales leaders in the managed print services business immediately implemented our advice and invested more time listening to calls being fielded by her company's customer support team. She quickly recognized that many of the calls coming in from customers could be prevented with clearer expectations set by her sales team.

The sales team brainstormed on how to prevent repeatable problems and questions being experienced by new clients. They embraced my philosophy that if a problem is repeatable, it's preventable. The sales team worked hard and created a better onboarding process for new clients. One step in the process included a videoconference with the new client and a member of the tech support team. During the meeting, they reviewed specific details such as delivery times and location of new equipment, even though those details had already been discussed with the salesperson. They brought up potential sales elephants that could occur with installation such as delays in delivery because a prior install took longer than expected.

The personal conversations between the new client and tech support team created an emotional connection and changed the conversation. The technician went from being just a voice on the phone or a signature line on an email. New clients liked putting a name to a face and were happy to be connecting with a live human being. Client happiness went up, as did client retention and referrals.

Sales managers, encourage other department managers to attend your sales meetings. On the outside, sales looks like a glamorous profession, filled with travel, expensive dinners, and golf. It's eye opening for other departments to learn the tenacity, courage, and hard work it takes to be successful in sales. Sitting in an airport for five hours and arriving home past midnight isn't glamorous. Hearing stories about aggressive competitors and the work it takes to compete and win business creates a healthy respect for the sales talent in the room.

Sales is not a department. It takes a sales village to win and retain business. Build your sales village and you will build better client relationships.

Sales Leaders EQ Action Plan

1. Encourage and support the development of sales and communication skills in other departments in the company.
2. Get out of the office. Invite other departments to join your sales team on calls with prospects and clients.
3. Examine your onboarding process for new clients. What repeatable problems are you encountering that could be prevented?
4. Build relationships with other departments in your company.
5. Preach and teach that sales is not a department. It takes a sales village to win and retain business.

21

Are You
Running Fake
Sales Meetings?

DO ANY OF THESE meeting scenarios look familiar to you?

It's the Monday morning group sales meeting. The sales team meanders in one by one. The sales meeting starts fifteen minutes late as the sales manager waits for everyone to show up.

Or, there's the sales meeting that is really a "Groundhog Day" meeting in disguise. The agenda never changes. It's a rote what's-in-your-pipeline sales meeting. The sales team gives excuses for stuck deals and extended closing dates. The meeting adjourns and the same deals are discussed the following week with the same excuses for not closing or moving forward.

Perhaps your sales meetings are really complaint meetings. The sales team shows up equipped to complain about everything that is wrong with the company. They make it clear that, until everything at the company is running perfectly, sales goals cannot be achieved.

What's wrong with this picture?

Everything!

A sales meeting that starts late sends a message to participants that the meeting really isn't that important. (It also sends a message that it's okay to show up late to sales calls.) Sales meetings aren't operations meetings or complaint meetings, they are sales meetings. These meetings are designed to do the hard work of mastering the skills and knowledge required to be a sales professional. Companies waste millions of dollars because they conduct fake sales meetings.

Sales meetings are designed for:

- *Team building.* But it's pretty hard to build teamwork when half the members of your sales team feel it's okay to show up late and waste other team members' valuable time.
- *Training and development.* Stop spending your time only on sales pipeline reviews. Focus time on giving your sales team better skills to *improve* their sales pipeline. They know how to read reports!
- *Brainstorming* on ways to up-level the service and expertise your sales team can provide to customers. Stop complaining about what the company isn't doing and control what you can control, which is exceptional client care.

Stop running average or below-average sales meetings. Add up the payroll in the room or on the conference call. That number should motivate you to get serious about running *great* sales meetings.

Get Clear on Your One Thing

Gary Keller is the author of the popular book *The One Thing.* In his book he shares a lot of great advice, one being his focusing question. "What's the one thing you can do such that by doing it, everything else will be easier or unnecessary?"

I was reminded of this question while listening to an interview conducted with Joel Osteen, pastor of Lakewood Church, a megachurch located in Houston, Texas. His televised sermons appear in more than ten million households. When asked how he manages this huge operation, he echoed Keller's one thing concept. He shared that his one thing—the most important thing—is the delivery of his sermon on Sunday. Pastor Osteen devotes a lot of time to this one thing. He researches material on Wednesday, writes the sermon on Thursday, memorizes it on Friday, and then delivers the sermon to two audiences on Saturday evening before the main, televised service on Sunday. He is clear about his one thing that leads to the continued success of Lakewood Church. His sermon on Sunday morning.

Sales managers, what if your one thing was preparing, running, and delivering *great* sales meetings? Not just good sales meetings, *great* sales meetings. What would become easier for your sales team? What would become easier for you?

Run Your Sales Meeting Like a Sales Meeting

Running an effective team sales meeting follows the same principles as conducting an effective sales meeting with prospects and customers.

You teach your sales team the importance of pre-call planning to ensure that meetings with prospects and customers are productive and relevant. You make sure your salespeople are running great meetings by asking questions such as:

- What is the purpose and objective of this meeting?
- What is your desired outcome?
- What resources do you need to conduct this meeting?

These are the exact same questions you should ask yourself to ensure your sales meetings are productive and relevant for the sales team:

- What is your purpose and objective for holding this sales meeting?
- What is your desired outcome? Are you trying to improve your sales team's selling skills? Is this meeting designed to motivate and inspire?
- What resources do you need to conduct this meeting? Do you have role-plays, practice sets, or games designed to test specific competencies? Do you need to review some movie clips or TED talks to provide motivation and inspiration?

Sales managers often express frustration because salespeople don't take the time to craft specific questions when meeting with prospects or clients. This lack of preparation leads to a "wing-it" sales call. But sales managers, you might be guilty of this same behavior. Have you put in the time to design questions that will create meaningful dialogue at your sales meeting? Or are you conducting "wing-it" sales meetings?

For example, you're going to introduce a new go-to-market strategy. Craft thought-provoking questions such as:

- Is this strategy in alignment with our core values?
- Is this a top priority for the quarter?
- If we do this, what initiatives will need to be placed on the back burner?
- How will this strategy provide value to our clients?
- How will this approach make us better than our competition?
- Is this the highest and best use of our time?

Good salespeople set clear next steps with prospects and customers. Good sales managers model the same behavior with their sales teams. After the sales meeting, send out correspondence summarizing action items discussed and agreed upon. Assign roles, responsibilities, and deadlines to be discussed at the next sales meeting.

Run your sales meeting like a sales meeting.

Invite the Experts

You don't have to be the only person providing your sales team with expertise and motivation.

Ask your CFO to a sales meeting and ask them to share what's important to them when making a buying decision. Your sales team will learn how a CFO thinks and measures a return on investment.

Invite a client to attend one of your sales meetings, in person or through videoconferencing. One of our clients invited one of their company's clients to jump on a conference call as part of a sales training meeting. It was really interesting to watch the sales team get fired up as the CIO shared her testimonial as to why she continued to work with their company. That sincere testimonial provided more "rah-rah" than any words I or the CEO could have provided that day.

How about inviting some top sales producers from a non-competing company to join your sales meeting and share their best practices for acquiring and retaining business? This sharing of best practices eliminates "it can't be done" thinking, because the ideas are coming from their peers. It also provides great networking and the possibility of building referral partnerships.

It's time to stop running fake sales meetings. Get clear on your one thing. Run *great* sales meetings, not just good sales meetings.

Sales Leaders EQ Action Plan

1. Get clear on your one thing. Conduct *great* sales meetings, not average sales meetings.

2. Determine your purpose and objective for each sales meeting. Get clear on your desired outcomes.
3. Apply delayed gratification skills. Put in the work of designing a great meeting. Plan questions, research TED talks, design effective role-plays.
4. Avoid vague next steps or no steps. Establish clear next steps based on sales meeting agenda and goals.
5. Invite other experts to share their wisdom.

22

What
Will
You Do?

FIRST OF ALL, THANK you for reading this book. Writing a book is similar to throwing a party. You wonder if anyone besides your relatives are going to show up or read the book.

Thank you for showing up to the party. I am humbled and appreciative because I know it's more comfortable to keep doing what you're doing. Learning new ideas, skills, and behaviors isn't easy. If it were, we'd all be very skinny millionaires.

I could end this book with motivational rhetoric such as the Nike slogan, "Just Do It." Or, "If it is to be it's up to me." But I won't because you know all the slogans and pithy quotes. Instead, I will simply pose the question: What will you do?

Will you continue to hire salespeople based on just their hard skills and statistics on their sales resume? Or, will you incorporate emotional intelligence skills into your hiring processes?

Will you expand your training and coaching sessions to include education around emotional intelligence skills? Or, will you settle for teaching the familiar sales techniques that you know so well?

Will you model the behaviors you expect from your sales team? Behaviors such as downtime, focus, empathy, and emotion management? Or, will you continue to model hurried and harried sales conversations and meetings?

Will you take time to build deeper relationships with clients and peers? Or, will you keep talking about the importance of relationships without making time for relationships?

Will you create sales meetings that educate and motivate? Or, will your sales meetings look more like a scene out of the movie *Groundhog Day?*

What will you do?

I've found life to be much more enjoyable as I continue on my journey to becoming a more emotionally intelligent person. Drama is reduced because of improved emotion management skills. (Yes, I am a recovering bull in a china shop.) Professional and personal relationships are better because of increased self-awareness and other awareness. Intentional downtime has decreased the number of empathy misses I make when holding conversations. My professional work is even more rewarding because of our unique approach in combining soft skills and hard skills training. I've had more than one salesperson and sales manager say to me that the integration of both has made achieving revenue goals easier and their job more enjoyable. That's a real win for me.

Please stay in touch. Connect with me on LinkedIn at www .linkedin.com/in/colleenstanleysli/. Or opt into our weekly vlog/blog with great sales and leadership tips, www.salesleadershipdevelopment .com/blog. Even better, give me a call at 877-287-0916. I'd welcome learning more about what you are doing to build an emotionally intelligent sales team.

It's time for a new perspective. It's time to incorporate emotional intelligence skills into your sales and leadership processes.

Index

About the Author

Colleen Stanley is president of SalesLeadership Inc. and has been in the sales development business for more than twenty years. She is the foremost expert and thought leader in bringing emotional intelligence to the sales profession. Salesforce named Colleen as one of the top eight influencers in sales of the twenty-first century. She is a popular speaker, author, and master trainer.